HEALING
THE
MASCULINE
SOUL

GORDON DALBEY

HEALING THE MASCULINE SOUL

An Affirming Message for Men
and
the Women Who Love Them

WORD PUBLISHING
Dallas · London · Vancouver · Melbourne

HEALING THE MASCULINE SOUL

Unless otherwise indicated, all Scripture quotations are from Today's English Version of the Bible, copyright © by the American Bible Society, 1966, 1971, 1976 and are used by permission.

The Holy Bible, New International Version (NIV). Copyright © 1973, 1978, 1984 International Bible Society. Used by permission of Zondervan Bible Publishers.

The New English Bible (NEB), copyright © the Delegates of the Oxford University Press and the Syndics of the Cambridge University Press, 1961, 1970. Reprinted by permission.

The Living Bible (TLB), copyright © 1971 by Tyndale House Publishers, Wheaton, IL. Used by permission.

The Revised Standard Version of the Bible (RSV), copyrighted 1946, 1952, © 1971, 1973 by the Division of Christian Education of the National Council of the Churches of Christ in the U.S.A., and used by permission.

Every effort has been made to trace the ownership of copyrighted material used in this book and to secure permission for its use. Should there be any inadvertent error or omission, the publishers will be pleased to make the necessary corrections in future printings.

Library of Congress Cataloging in Publication Data

Dalbey, Gordon, 1944–
  Healing the masculine soul.

  Bibliography: p.
  1. Men—Psychology. 2. Masculinity (Psychology)
3. Sex role. 4. Men—Religious life. I. Title.
BF692.5.D35 1988   155.6'32   88-17679
ISBN 0-8499-0664-4

Printed in the United States of America

01239 RRD 9876

This book is dedicated to my father,
who taught me by example to value
integrity, to search beyond appearances
after truth, to appreciate life as a
gift from God, and therefore, to find
its meaning in serving others.

Contents

Introduction: Recognizing the Wound   9

1   The Lion Speaks   25

2   Out from the Womb   35

3   Come Out, Son of Our People!   49

4   She Left Me!   59

5   From Love Bug to Faith:
Sexuality and Spirituality   80

6   To Corral the Stallion   89

7   Lost Among Men:
A Nonpolitical View of Homosexuality   102

8   Warrior Redeemed   117

9   Boots for a Working Man   130

10   The Father and the Man:
Of Sons and Daughters   145

11   To Know the Father   161

12   Where Are All the Men?:
Why Men Don't Come to Church   174

13   Rational and Independent, Faithless and Alone   188

14   An Ancient Mama's Boy Is Called Out:
Wrestling with the Father God for New Life   202

Epilogue: The Mirror of Truth   207

Endnotes   211

Introduction: Recognizing the Wound

TODAY IN MY MID-FORTIES I span a history which has challenged painfully my sense of manhood. A "war baby," I grew up playing sandlot soldier in my white suburban neighborhood with boys whose mothers were all "housewives." After graduating from a private, then-segregated university in 1964, I went to Africa as a Peace Corps volunteer and later taught at a junior high school in the Hispanic *barrio* of San Jose, California. By the seventies, I had become an enthusiastic supporter of civil rights, women's liberation, and the antiwar movement. In effect, I had become part of a generation of men who actively rejected our childhood macho image of manhood—which seemed to us the cornerstone of racism, sexism, and militarism.

The seventies, however, offered us no model of authentic manhood sufficiently inspiring to supplant the boyhood image in our hearts. Lacking that, we could only reject our manhood itself as we rejected the macho image.

By the eighties, alienated from our masculine heritage and intimidated by a growing host of strong women, we have become fearfully lost and vulnerable in the very culture we struggled to foster years ago. We realize that in rejecting the macho image, we have gained a deeper sensitivity to other persons. But as we approach the nineties, we wonder what we have lost.

In talking with other men about this, I have encountered widespread agreement. At the same time, I find myself increasingly frustrated with the scarcity of resources which speak to our common needs as men today. The overwhelming majority of books dealing with sexuality and identity in our time are aimed at women: *Fathers and Daughters; My Mother, My Self; Men Who Hate Women and the Women Who Love Them; Smart Women, Foolish Choices; Women Who Love Too Much*, to name a few.

Clearly, women buy more books than men, and publishers are quick to capitalize on that. "In these books," as author Howard Halpern notes, "men—immature, impossible, and self-centered—are the villains." Indeed, referring to his own book, *How to Break Your Addiction to a Person*, Halpern declares that, although it has sold well among both sexes, "I have always known that if I had called it *How to Break Your Addiction to the Wrong Man*, it would sell two or three times as much."

To his credit, Halpern did not yield to such a temptation, "for two reasons":

First, the problem of being trapped by a destructive, frustrating or unfulfilling relationship they cannot leave is shared by both men and women. Second, I did not want to contribute to the negative atmosphere created by those male-bashing books. It doesn't do men any good to be defined as bad, immature, wrong, women-haters, "rats," etc., and it's a disservice to women to define them as either helpless or constantly fighting to avoid victimization by their lovers or spouses.[1]

Halpern is to be commended for not joining what he calls the current "male-bashing bonanza" among book publishers. At the same time, any sensitive male knows that we men today share in a great deal of brokenness. Certainly, we may cling to "addictive" relationships as fearfully as women, and perhaps for the same reasons, such as a fear of loneliness and rejection. But common diagnosis does not require uniform prescription. As the medicine and treatment must be tailored to each individual's body chemistry and lifestyle, so a prescription for healing the man must be based upon the male nature and experience.

I did find several books aimed exclusively at men. Yet, as a man who views my masculinity—as all aspects of life—from the perspective of Christian spirituality, I found myself ultimately frustrated with these "male-oriented" books. The secular ones simply offered no spiritual perspective at all, while the Christian ones confined themselves largely to exhortation, ignoring both psychological insights and spiritual experience.

In the Bible, however, godly exhortation finds its mark only *after* encounter with the Living God. The Ten Commandments, for example, are given in the wilderness context of God's acting to save His people. Hence, God introduces the commandments not with a half-time pep talk to win the battle against sin, but rather, with a reminder of His authority *by virtue of that saving encounter:*

> I am the Lord your God who brought you out of Egypt, where you were slaves. Worship no god but me (Ex. 20:1).

Needed, therefore, was a book portraying not only our real-life problems as men today, but also the God whose word is "alive and active" (Heb. 4:12) even now, who is struggling with and for us to find solutions—and who confirms His written word through dreams, visions, parables, prophecies, and the entire range of biblical spirituality. As the apostle reminded the early men of the Church:

> Our brothers, we know that God loves you and has chosen you to be his own. For we brought the Good News to you, not with words only, but also with power and the Holy Spirit. (1 Thess. 1:4, 5).

Above all, therefore, we need to know and draw close to the God who has demonstrated unto death and resurrection that He will both stand with us where we are and lead us into new life as well.

But to let God meet us where we are, we must know where we are. And such an exercise in truth-telling can often be painful.

We must distinguish here between a "male-basher" and a Christian truth-teller, according to one's goal. The former may seek revenge, or to portray the woman as superior. But for the Christian, the truth must be spoken "in a spirit of love" (Eph. 4:15), so that the body be built up, the relationship be restored, the community affirmed (v. 16). The faithful truth-teller, like Jesus on the cross, does not surrender to a spirit of either vengeance or pride—but rather, to the God who alone heals through death unto life, who instructs the yielded heart when to move in compassion, and when to confront.

The most succinct and faithful portrayal of our problem as men today—balancing both hard truth and hopeful compassion, offering both secular and spiritual remedy—I found in a short article pointedly titled, "Healing the Tear in the Masculine Soul," by Ted Dobson, a Catholic priest. Declaring that men today have "excluded themselves from the most important issues of life," Dobson enumerates:

> Often they are not active members of their own families, unable to have effective relationships with significant others, and unknowledgeable about how to rear their children. They often separate themselves from religion—that is, from developing a relationship with the center of the universe. They are often emotionally undeveloped, and their ability to care for and be cared for is stunted. They often recoil from personal growth; many a counselor will report that in marriage difficulties the male rarely sees any problems in himself, that he refuses to admit any responsibility for the problems, and that he especially refuses to change.

Dobson traces this brokenness in men to the fact that boys lack sufficient contact with their fathers to generate a healthy masculine self-image. Indeed, in a brilliant insight, he says that the essential macho characteristic of appearing "remote" simply reflects the remoteness of fathers from their sons. If the father defines masculinity for the boy, that is, a father who is distant physically and/or emotionally from his son, communicates that manliness is a matter of standing aloof from others.

Such enforced alienation stunts a man's spiritual growth:

> Spiritually, faith is considered by many men at the most to be a personal matter of which they would rarely talk, but more often to be a woman's area of concern, for it implies a lack of independence and self-assurance that does not coincide with their macho self-image.

Dobson concludes:

> There is a "tear" in the masculine soul—a gaping hole or wound that leads to a profound insecurity. The German psychologist, Alexander Mitscherlich, has written that society has torn the soul of the male, and into this tear demons have fled—demons of insecurity, selfishness, and despair. Consequently, men do not know who they are as men. Rather, they define themselves by what they do, who they know, or what they own.

The hope which Dobson proclaims is precisely that of our faith:

> As we bring our insecurity, unforgiveness, and immature thought/behavior patterns to the Lord honestly and vulnerably, He can free us from our pain and weakness and both lead and empower us to live a new way.

Acknowledging that "for most men" such an "inner journey" is "yet a foreign territory," Dobson nevertheless offers a powerful vision of a society of men who have thus dared to let God heal them of "the tear in their masculine souls":

> Unfortunately for themselves, their families, and their communities, (men) have been satisfied with surface definitions of their

masculinity, and have not probed the wonders of their deep masculine selves. Were they to choose to do so, our world would be a much different place, for men would be able once again to truly lead, guide, and direct their own lives and others'. They would be able to carry their fair share of the burdens of our human and Christian communities. They would once again be truly able to enjoy their lives, not in selfishness, but in the wonder of contributing their strength for the well-being of others.[2]

Excited by Dobson's words even as they convicted me, I found myself wishing for a more comprehensive resource, a book which would portray both the tear in our masculine souls and God's power to heal it.

My own thoughts crystallized when, in seeking "male" resources, I came upon my local school district's adult education catalog. Searching hopefully through the "Self-Help and Improvement" section, I was struck by the rich variety of listings aimed at women. Some were named directly after a book, such as "Smart Women, Foolish Choices," while others proclaimed broader concerns, such as "Assertiveness Training for Women." Even the aerobics classes, with their exhortations to "flatten your tummy and firm up those thighs," were clearly aimed at women.

The catalog listed no course designed explicitly for men.

Frustrated over this apparent lack of concern for men's needs, it occurred to me that I myself might offer such a course. Certainly, I had to consider the likelihood that no such course existed simply because no men really wanted one. Yet my own struggles and those of the men I knew testified convincingly that, whether or not we men *want* to get together and share our needs, we clearly *need* to. Our collective pain over marital problems, job uncertainties, confusion in fathering, self-doubts and the like, cries out for an audience of fellow men—brothers in both suffering and hope, fellow soldiers battling together after victory.

I decided that a secular audience would be the best testing ground for my ideas, out of the biblical understanding that the nonbeliever is better qualified to judge whether or not an activity manifests the authentic presence of God (1 Cor. 14:24, 25). One's own family is often too easy an audience.

And so I wrote to the principal of the local adult education school, expressing my concern for men's needs and outlining a proposed course to address those needs, titled, "For Men Only: Reclaiming Manhood in the Modern Age." I had tailored my proposal around four basic roles by which most of us judge our masculinity: son of the father, warrior, lover of a woman, and provider.

From the outset, I felt it best to exclude women from the course. Most men, I assumed, have shared more of their honest feelings and needs with women than with other men. Women are simply more receptive to such sharing, more skilled in it—and therefore might too readily dominate the discussions. Our problem today as men is not that we have failed to bond with a woman, but rather, with our own, manly selves. If indeed we have failed to bond with a woman, it is because we have not first bonded with our own manhood—recognized, accepted, celebrated, employed it. In the course, I did not want to short-circuit our modern-day fear of the masculine—reflected in our fear of other men—but rather, to face it, to experience it, and in such a controlled classroom environment, to gain victory over it.

Without having thus bonded with his own masculine self, I believe that a man's effort to bond with a woman, as in marriage, can only be an escape from this, his true self.

At the same time, my enlightened sensitivities balked. Was a class "For Men Only" simply another effort to exclude women as a reflection of male pride and control? I decided it was not. For my course was designed to help men become strong enough in their own manly selves to affirm women in their feminine selves, and thereby, to be less threatened by them.

Nevertheless, I knew that any public school programming today would be bound by legal restraints against sexism, and when the principal finally invited me for an interview to present my course proposal, I prepared an extensive argument in its behalf. Indeed, I recall entering his office both uncertain and uneasy.

Setting my several thick files of newspaper clippings, magazine articles, bibliographies, and the like on his desk, I shook his
hand gingerly and sat down.

"Well, Mr. Dalbey, I'm glad to meet you," he said quickly,
with an enthusiasm that surprised me. Almost before I could
respond, he had pulled out a large course-scheduling sheet. "Now,
when would you like me to schedule your course?" he invited,
pen poised.

Startled by such immediate receptivity, I hesitated. "Oh,
I . . . uh, that is . . . Thursday nights," I replied. Catching myself, I reached very casually for my files and drew them onto my
lap and out of sight. "Yes, the first four Thursday evenings of the
term would be fine," I declared, shaking my head and smiling
engagingly as he penned in the dates.

Amazing! I thought. *No third-degree questioning, no reserva-
tion whatsoever!*

Within five minutes, the principal had secured my class in the
upcoming schedule and was thanking me profusely for my interest
in his school. Realizing that I had nothing to lose, I decided to ask
him directly why he was so quick to accept my course proposal.

"I must confess I'd prepared quite an argument for my
course, expecting you'd balk at it for excluding women," I said.
"Frankly, I'm curious why you were so . . . receptive to it."

"Well . . . ," he began, hesitating. "We've been having a
few questions lately from federal examiners."

Puzzled, I shrugged my shoulders. "I guess I don't understand what you mean."

"You know, questions over sex discrimination in our
courses," he said.

"Now you've got me even more baffled," I confessed. "That's
just what I was afraid of—that you might run into trouble for
having a course for men only."

"No, no," he exclaimed amiably. "I don't mean discrimination against women, but against *men*. The problem is that we have
so many courses for women only and nothing at all for men. With
your course, we can at last show the federal examiners that we're
making an effort to balance that out."

I shook my head in amazement. "Wow—the pendulum has really swung, hasn't it?!"

Smiling thinly, he nodded. "We'll be looking forward to your course."

In the weeks prior to the first class, I sent out over two hundred course announcements to clergy, social workers, therapists, and community groups. In addition, the course was advertised in the regular adult school catalog. Still, only eight men showed up.

Disappointed at the low turnout, I nevertheless reminded myself that my course idea was a relatively new one, and had been prompted precisely because men were not inclined to get together this way.

Furthermore, the broad range of men represented was encouraging: in age, from twenty-nine to sixty-seven; in profession, from printer to engineer; in education, from high school to graduate degree; in religion, from "born again" Christian to Jew to "none." Over the four weeks, these men shared with increasing vulnerability and intensity stories about mothers, fathers, jobs, children, wives, and hopes. At the end of the last session, they asked if we could meet for an all-day Saturday session.

In quality, if not quantity, the course was an overwhelming success. The need I had sensed among men was indeed there, and the pain and fear which it prompted in each man was noticeably eased as we dared draw closer to one another in trust.

The major loose end, the essential unfinished business of the course emerged as early as the second session, when one man exclaimed, "Now that we all realize we didn't get what we needed from our fathers, what can we do about it?" Recognizing my limitations in a secular environment, I pointed out the collective sense of relief we all experienced in sharing openly with each other our need for fatherly care.

"One thing we can all do is commit ourselves to reaching out to other men to make friendships and talk more together about our real needs," I said. And then, pausing, I realized that my own integrity called for a further response. "For me, the answer to your question can only come out of an intentional relationship with the God who I believe created you and is calling you even now into true manhood among fellow men." I then simply invited any who wanted to pursue that idea to see me after the class.

By the end of the course, I had received abundant confirmation of its importance from "unbelievers," and I began to pray for opportunities to minister to Christian men. I sent out a flyer on my "For Men Only" course, tailored for churches, to three hundred clergy and waited. For several months, I received no response. But as always, I began to sense that the Lord was using this time to prepare me in His perspective.

I first realized this following a church showing of the anti-abortion film, "The Silent Scream." Deeply touched by the film, the audience of perhaps a hundred persons, both men and women, moved into prayer. When the pastor invited individual prayers aloud, one person prayed for the young pregnant women; others prayed for the parents of these women, for the doctors and nurses at abortion clinics, for the unborn babies themselves, and for the nation's conscience. As I sat, head bowed, my spirit agreed with all these prayers. And yet, a restless uneasiness prodded me. Something was missing, overlooked. "Lord," I prayed, "is there something else, something perhaps even more key to the issue than all those being mentioned?"

Almost at once the words burst forth in my mind: "Pray for the men! No one is recognizing that without a man to impregnate the woman, the abortion issue would not exist. The men are the problem, and no one even recognizes the need for My transforming hand upon them. Even if a woman agrees or even seeks sexual intercourse, she cannot force herself upon the man. It is he who has the ultimate responsibility to say no, and it is he whom I therefore hold ultimately accountable."

"Lord," I prayed, "How shall I pray for the men?"

In my heart, I sensed a clear answer. "The men are not submitted to Me. They have become passive in the face of responsibility. They are not living in response to Me; it is in that sense that they have given up the ability to respond, that is, their response-ability. Pray that the men surrender to Me, that they would receive

My heart of caring for women, that the spirit of passivity would be bound over them and they would walk in responsibility."

When I spoke this prayer aloud, a unanimous murmur of approval and amens! swept the room.

Some time after, I was invited to a churchmen's breakfast featuring an antipornography film in which Christian educator James Dobson warned—often in frightening detail—against the growing tide of smut available in our society today. Though the film itself showed nothing but Dr. Dobson talking from his podium, at times in his talk I found myself startled by lustful thoughts which flashed in my mind.

After the film, the men rose up in one voice to condemn pornography and commit themselves to eliminating such magazines, films, and the like from our community.

Yet, amid this stirring oratory and unanimous call to arms, I found myself balking. Certainly, I agreed that pornography is patently evil and repugnant to God, that children of God should indeed work to eliminate it. But even as I longed to join in the outcry about me, I knew that the Lord was calling me to proclaim a deeper, and hence, more lasting vision of victory.

As I prayed for understanding—*Lord, what is this check in my spirit?*—I sensed that the Lord had allowed those lustful thoughts to flash in my mind to remind me that pornography is the symptom of a deeper brokenness in men today. With rare exceptions, the overwhelming bulk of smut produced today is bought by men, not women. To eliminate the filthy symptom without healing the brokenness that seeks it, is not full and lasting victory in the Lord.

"Lord," I asked, "what has happened to men that we would seek such evil? What brokenness do we bear that has led us to seek saving power in pornography, instead of in You? Where have we lost the deep and abiding sense of our healthy masculine sexuality that we would turn to so sick a substitute?"

A war has many battles; a campaign, many fronts. Let us by all means battle pornography. But in doing so, let us not ignore the primary front itself, namely, the wound in the masculine soul.

Several weeks after viewing the antipornography film, I received a call from a woman who directs a local consortium of resources for victims of "domestic violence." As she described their referral agencies, I was genuinely impressed and encouraged that this growing problem might be significantly arrested through their hotlines, shelter facilities, teen pregnancy services, emergency counseling for rape victims, family support groups, and medical aid for battered women.

Yet again, I balked.

"As a minister, I really appreciate and support all your efforts to minister to victims of violence," I said. "But you know, in the majority of cases, it's a man who commits the violence, and I'm concerned that your resources all focus on the victims, and none deal with helping the perpetrator change his ways."

"Well, of course, it's the victim who comes for help," she noted matter-of-factly. "You just don't often find the man who beats his wife and children coming and asking for help."

"I know," I sighed. "You're absolutely right. But still . . . I'm just concerned that nobody is trying to reach the men. It's like the house is flooded and everyone's struggling with buckets and mops, but nobody's trying to fix the broken pipe!"

As I reflected on these three growing agendas of social reform—abortion, pornography, domestic violence—I realized that even the major agendas of the mainline liberal churches (peace, poverty, and women's liberation) also bear directly upon men. Not only do men impregnate women with unwanted babies, buy pornography, and commit violence in homes; we also make wars, hold the seats of financial power, and resist equal opportunity for women.

Clearly, the Church, both conservative and liberal, is manifestly concerned about these important issues, each of which essentially demands a change in male behavior. Yet meanwhile—can it be mere coincidence?—relatively few men actually participate in church life. Only about a third of church members, according to a recent survey, are men. In fact, over half of the students in mainline church seminaries today are women, and that figure is increasing.

There is, however, one major institution today in which those figures are reversed, which draws a far greater percentage of men than women: prisons. Why are so many men in prison and so few in church?

Clearly, the answer lies within the tear in the masculine soul—which the churches have largely ignored, which the prisons can house but not heal.

Could this "tear" be traced to efforts—both our own, and those of society—to tear us away from the macho image of manhood? If so, its healing requires that we reexamine ourselves and that image with new eyes—indeed, with the very sensitivity and compassion which we have ostensibly gained in our season of liberation.

Certainly, we men do not fantasize before *Playboy* centerfolds because we are so courageous before real-live, three-dimensional women, but rather, because we fear them; we do not beat up women because we are so strong, but rather, because we feel so powerless before them; we do not impregnate women and leave them to consider an abortion because we are so self-reliant, but rather, because we feel inadequate to be responsible fathers and husbands.

In a word, our masculine soul is torn—so badly that we cannot recognize the One who comes to heal us.

In the Christian tradition, the diabolic is not wholly independent of the divine, but rather, a perversion of it—a fallen angel, a counterfeit. What if the macho image is diabolic not because it is categorically evil, but because it presumes upon the true and good nature of authentic manliness—and distorts that?

If so, our task as men today is not to curse our manhood, but to redeem it, in the true prophetic sense.

For example, in the sixties men were exhorted to "make love, not war." In the context of sexual relationships today, men might readily interpret this to mean, "Be noncombative with the woman." Yet twenty years later, in the eighties, the educated, ambitious women I know are chewing up such men and spitting them out, even as they long for a man to stand up to them and offer a credible counterpoint worthy of their respect.

What if, instead of either making love or war, we men need to recognize an appropriate time to be firm and unyielding before the woman, as well as to court her? What if we men need to face the authentic life battles at hand, victory in which demands response to a calling that is higher than coupling with the woman, and more ultimately persuasive than violence?

If so, we men have a tough job ahead—but one at last wholly worthy of our manly energies.

As in any battle, we cannot escape the consequences of retreat. If we men shrink from this awesome task of redeeming the manhood which beckons us, if we abdicate the struggle to articulate an authentic manhood with not only words and deeds, but with new images as well, the old demons of violence and lust will surely attack with a vengeance.

But where shall we men today find the authentic images to guide us in our godly redemption as men—that is, the stories which will enable us to recognize the ancient biblical story and its God as our own, even today?

What if those stories are among us, even within us, longing to be told?

HEALING
THE
MASCULINE
SOUL

1
The
Lion
Speaks

When a lion roars, who can keep from being afraid? When the Sovereign Lord speaks, who can keep from proclaiming his message? (Amos 3:8)

SEVERAL YEARS AGO, a friend and fellow pastor held me spellbound as he told me about a man in his parish who had come to him distraught over a terrifying recurrent dream, in which a ferocious lion kept chasing the man until he dropped exhausted and awoke screaming. Assuming that the lion represented something fearful in the man's life, my friend offered several possibilities: the man's boss? wife? some heavy responsibility?

As they discussed each, the man became increasingly frustrated. Yes, all of these bore some fear for him, but no one of them with enough conviction to be the entire focus of this relentless nightmare. Frustrated and uncertain, my friend decided finally to pray with the man for a clearer sense of what was happening. He began the prayer as usual, asking for the Father God's love and protection, for Jesus to be present, and for the Holy Spirit to provide every gift of knowledge and wisdom needed.

As they prayed, my friend on impulse invited the man to recall the dream, even in all its fear. Hesitantly, the man agreed, and soon reported that indeed, the lion was in sight and headed his way. My friend then instructed the man, "When the lion comes close to you, try not to run away, but instead, stand there and ask him who or what he is, and what he's doing in your life. I'll be praying for you—can you try that?"

Shifting uneasily in his chair, the man agreed, then reported what was happening: "The lion is snorting and shaking his head, standing right there in front of me. . . . I ask him who he is . . . and—Oh! I can't believe what he's saying! He says, 'I'm your courage and your strength. Why are you running away from me?'"

Puzzled at first—whatever could this mean, for a man to be *afraid* of his courage and strength?—I was nevertheless utterly fascinated, and seized by this story with an intensity which seemed both personal and universal. Today, through working and praying with numerous men, teaching courses for men only, and allowing the Lord to show me a deeper view of my own self, I have become convinced that this dream-story of the man running away from his own lion-hearted courage and strength is a parable for men of our time.

At the most basic level, the story reminds us that authentic manhood seeks men, and is not something we ourselves properly seek. It is bestowed, not seized, lest it be fabricated.

For too long, the image of manhood in our culture has been corrupted by the model of the "seeker," the perpetually dissatisfied lone-wolf cowboy, space-jockey, motorcycle rider. The one primarily oriented toward seeking, however, is most likely to hold in his mind, even subconsciously, an image of the object or state of mind he desires. The seeker's focus, or lifestyle orientation, tends to reflect his own self-serving human nature instead of God's image or desire for him.

In our secular culture, advertising is quick to provide such human-centered goal images: the truck, the cigar, the beer, the bikini model. But the very vitality of advertising is based upon our dissatisfaction and insecurity, for the securely satisfied customer stops buying. The world therefore fears the man who is secure in his manhood, because he cannot be manipulated into buying its trucks and beer as a means of securing it.

We males could not so eagerly embrace such a surrogate manhood with its frustrating dissatisfaction unless the genuine article frightened us. The lion dream-image, indeed, suggests that authentic manhood is a fearful thing, that we males today—even as we long to be "real men"—are afraid of the courage and strength it bears.

For courage has no meaning apart from danger—nor strength apart from weakness. To be given courage and strength implies the responsibility to exercise them. Are we prepared for that?

Ability does not necessarily imply eagerness to exercise it. While growing up in school, for example, I was several years younger than my classmates and hence, shorter. My below-average playground performance made me think that I could not compete athletically. For years after graduating from college, even when I was a muscular 5'10", I still shied away from competitive sports. As I saw my abilities improve, however, I found myself struggling against a fear of playing well.

To this day, I am relaxed and enjoy tennis when the score is relatively even, and can overlook it when I lose. But when I am holding "set point," I tense up. Once, after being ahead several games with a friend of no better ability than my own, I lost the set.

"You surprised me, coming from behind like that," I remarked afterward.

"Actually, I knew you wouldn't win," he said matter-of-factly, "because I could tell you didn't expect to."

That stung. When I prayed about it later, I saw my pattern:

if you always lose, losing can be passed off as a lifestyle instead of a defeat. Knowing that "I am a loser," protected me from the pain of defeat; knowing later that I might win, however, opened the door on a whole new world—as terrifying as it was promising.

So I ran from the lion, and lost the set.

Furthermore, the dream-image itself, as a vehicle for these truths, beckons the spiritual dimension to manhood, its uncontainable mystery. Unlike Third World men, who recognize and respond out of spiritual reality, we "modern-scientific" men have fearfully avoided facing spiritual power, because it shatters our treasured goal-image of rational self-sufficiency. In our God-created hearts, we know that genuine manhood is rooted in mysteries which no logic or computer program can comprise. The spiritual dimension to manhood thereby reminds us of our inadequacy, and we prefer to ignore if not suppress it altogether.

What if, indeed, authentic manhood can be approached only in relationship with the Father God, who seeks in every man to fulfill the purpose for which He has created him? If so, true manhood is not something to be sought, but to be revealed, precisely as a man submits to the God who called him into being and in whom lies his ultimate destiny. Indeed, because God's ways threaten our self-centeredness, we fear authentic manhood in Him as we cling to our own plans and desires.

Years ago, when I taught at an inner-city junior high school, I came upon an angry scene in which one boy was challenging another to a fight. "He's callin' you out!" others yelled to the one challenged.

What if the essential nature of manhood is revealed as our Creator God "calls us out," even to frightening occasions of conflict, challenge, and risk—even to struggle against Himself, and His desires for us? If so, then "response-able" manhood is defined by a man's readiness to respond to that call.

This is not to advocate that we men go around seeking fights, but that we be prepared to respond when God reveals to us the fight which He has equipped us to win.

While teaching at a suburban private boys' high school, I talked with one particularly meek senior who had taken up karate lessons. "It gives me some confidence to know that if some other kid tries to put me down, I could kill him," he declared. Searching for a way to help him recognize the sham in that confidence, I asked if in fact he were now more at peace around other boys. "Well," he confessed, "actually it's more like now I'm hoping to pick a fight, so I can prove what I can do."

Gently, I suggested that in spite of his karate lessons, he still had not dealt with his basic insecurity as a young man—much of which seemed rooted in his absentee father—and expressed my concern that his anxiety to avoid confronting that insecurity might lead him into conflict to which God had not called him, and hence, which might be quite harmful to himself and others.

Destructive power destroys—even the one who wields it. Satan cannot cast out Satan. He who lives by the sword, dies by the sword—because to live by the sword is to give one's life over to death.

The fact that this young man based his "confidence" among other men upon his ability to destroy them not only indicates his terrible fear of other men, but also suggests the apocryphal nature of that confidence, and its source in darkness.

It's hard for us men to form close relationships with one another; hence, one author's title, *The Friendless American Male.*[1] What, indeed, are we so afraid of in other men that keeps us so alienated from one another? On the surface, it would appear that we are afraid other men will destroy us, hence the term, "the manly art of self-defense." In fact, however, I believe we are afraid of the manly courage and strength which is summoned when we men come together.

I believe that a unique and truly awesome power arises when men gather together: the power which God gives especially to men collectively, to get His work done in this world. Yet, because this power is so much greater than my own individual self, my ego is threatened by it. My self-centered human nature assumes that power originates in the other men and not God; because I know I cannot measure up to it myself, I judge myself as less "manly" than the others. My ego perceives that power as destructive, and prepares me to defend against it—instead of to join with it.

Even as we misperceive the lion, therefore, I believe that what we truly experience among other men is not the power to destroy, but to create—the pure courage and strength which God manifests in the masculine. Our fear of lost ego blinds us to this primal truth, and thereby invites the power of the destroyer to supplant the power of the Creator in our relationships with other men.

Hence, wars.

The major component of this power which God engenders among men is simply the Word of truth. As author Leanne Payne has noted, "The power to honor the truth—to speak it and *be* it—is at the heart of true masculinity."[2]

Thus, we speak of a manly "integrity," or "strength of character." The biblical faith, in fact, portrays this power with the masculine image of a sword:

> The word of God is alive and active, sharper than any double-edged sword. It cuts all the way through, to where soul and spirit meet, to where joints and marrow come together. It judges the desires and thoughts of a man's heart. There is nothing that can be hid from God; everything in all creation is exposed and lies open before his eyes. And it is to him that we must all give an account of ourselves (Heb. 4:12, 13).

This is indeed a fearful Presence, particularly as we hide from the truth about ourselves. It does indeed spell death to the ego; the ego-bound man, unsubmitted to God, can only perceive it as destructive.

And so we run from the lion.

Most men recognize that truth-telling requires courage and that lying betrays fear and cowardice. Societies that suppress the truth may rightly be seen as unmanly; that explains American men's stand for freedom and against communism as an apparent measure of their manhood.

Yet, in order to claim any manliness in comparison to the cowardly deceits of communistic systems, we American men must be willing to apply the same standard of truth to ourselves. And all too often, the "manly art of self-defense" becomes the unmanly enterprise of defending ourselves from the truth of our wrong-doings—as in the Watergate "cover-up," the ITT and other business scams, sports pay-offs and drug use, and union featherbedding.

If truth is the power which God invests primarily in masculinity, then we fear being with other men because together the uncomfortable truths about us shall be revealed. Only as we surrender our self-centered pride to God, therefore, can we begin to base our confidence among other men not upon our own ability to destroy, but upon God's ability to create. Instead of defending ourselves from the truth, we can appropriate the courage and strength we share, and work together to improve our common welfare.

Hence, peace.

My karate-wielding student, for example, knew that among other men, God's spirit of truth would reveal his physical and emotional weakness. His fear of rejection convinced him that his greatest danger lay in being called out by other men, and he was preparing himself to destroy any who might. He therefore hoped to defend the secret truth of his inner fears and self-doubts from other men by using a physical strength they would respect. Yet he thereby gave other men, struggling with their own fears, the power to define his manhood, and thus sold his birthright as a son of God for a few karate chops.

His deep natural longing for esteem in the eyes of men overshadowed his deeper spiritual longing for esteem in the eyes of the Father God. For the true man of God, as defined by the biblical faith, does not seek first to please other men. Such shameless submission to others belies the dignity which men respect. "After all," as Paul admonished the brothers in Rome,

> who is a real Jew, truly circumcised? It is not the man who is a Jew on the outside, whose circumcision is a physical thing. Rather, the real Jew is the person who is a Jew on the inside, and this is the work of God's Spirit, not of the written Law. Such a person receives his praise from God, not from man (Rom. 2:28, 29).

We men today fear most not being called out by other men, but being called out by God, who in Jesus has promised to raise

His sword against our self-centered human nature. For Jesus is the Word of truth who nails our proud flesh to the cross—who calls us to accountability in order to redeem and restore us to His image of righteousness. As with the lion dream, we may run from the painful truth which God bears. But ultimately, no man can outrun God. As the psalmist proclaimed,

> Lord, you have examined me and you know me. You know every-thing I do. . . . Where could I go to escape from you? Where could I get away from your presence? If I went up to heaven, you would be there; if I lay down in the world of the dead, you would be there (Ps. 139:1, 7, 8).

Significantly, although the psalmist fears God's power as it holds him forever accountable for his sins, he celebrates it as the same power that gives him protection and life itself:

> You are all around me on every side; you protect me with you. power. . . . You created every part of me; you put me together in my mother's womb. I praise you because you are to be feared; all you do is strange and wonderful. I know it with all my heart (139:5, 13, 14).

And so at last, he yields—not in terror, but in hope of being drawn at last into God's eternal righteousness:

> Examine me, O God, and know my mind; test me, and discover my thoughts. Find out if there is any evil in me and guide me in the everlasting way (139:23, 24).

Dare we, like the psalmist and the man who brought his dream to my pastor friend, give up and let the lion have his way in our lives at last? When we have exhausted all our own resources in running from Him, dare we cry out—not screaming in terror for the loss of pride and self, but weeping pent-up tears of longing for the courage and strength we have feared to receive?

If, indeed, God is a loving Father who wants to bring His sons into the courage and strength of manhood, what shall He do when He has called us out and we do not respond—when we do not exercise response-ability? The biblical answer is clear: He shall destroy our hiding place. As Jeremiah prophesied against those who attempted to hide from their sins in the temple itself:

> You steal, murder, commit adultery, tell lies under oath, offer sacrifices to Baal, and worship gods that you had not known before. You do these things I hate, and then you come and stand in my presence, in my own Temple, and say, "We are safe!" Do you think that my Temple is a hiding place for robbers? . . . And so, what I did to Shiloh I will do to this Temple of mine, in which you trust. . . . I will drive you out of my sight (Jer. 7:9–11, 14, 15).

Our modern temples of humanly defined manhood must fall; everything on which we base our manhood, besides God, must be taken from us: the woman, the job, the esteem of other men. For God declared to His people:

> I will abandon my people until they have suffered long enough for their sins and come looking for me. Perhaps in their suffering they will try to find me (Hosea 5:15).

Such is the love of the Father:

> Of all the nations on earth, you are the only one I have known and cared for. That is what makes your sins so terrible, and that is why I must punish you for them (Amos 3:2).

Very likely, the reader concerned enough to buy a book on masculine strength has experienced the kind of loss which drives men to seek God at last and to discover His mercy. Those men who are returning from such "exile" and its "discipline of disaster"[3]—perhaps through being divorced, fired, or scorned by other men—must know that even now seeking God's courage and strength among other men remains difficult, for the opposition remains among us.

In our fallen world, to give oneself to God and to recognize the power He has given us together as His sons, is to encounter opposition. Men still crucify the one who bears the Word of their salvation; we may be called "wimps," or be regarded as "religious nuts." So we must be equipped for conflict as well as creation as were Nehemiah's men, who carried swords along with the bricks with which they rebuilt the temple.

Our own weapons in this post-Easter age, however, will not be like their swords, for the victorious, risen Christ has revealed at last the true, spiritual battle in which we are engaged. Thus, the apostle declared:

> It is true that we live in the world, but we do not fight from worldly motives. The weapons we use in our fight are not the world's weapons but God's powerful weapons, which we use to destroy strongholds. We destroy false arguments; we pull down every proud obstacle that is raised against the knowledge of God; we take every thought captive and make it obey Christ (2 Cor. 10:3-5).

Our sword will be of the Spirit, not of steel. And it is this sword of God's truth, tempered by the fire of our suffering and sharpened against His hard-rock determination to shape us in His image of the truth that sets men free.

Biblical faith proclaims that it is a fearful thing to fall into the hands of the Living God, for we discover there—and only there—the absolute worthlessness of our own human power.

So we run from the lion.

Yet only in such submission, as at the cross, do we discover at last the absolute worth of God's power—and His longing for us to walk in it.

If, that is, we dare to respond as God calls us out to become His men, if we allow Him to nail our pride and our plans to the Cross, we are eligible at last to receive the Father God's Spirit and do our appointed part toward restoring His kingdom on earth as it is in heaven.

Growing faithfully toward such an emotional and spiritual goal requires a man to face squarely the most basic reality of physical life in this world—and also, as we shall now see, the greatest threat to his masculine development.

2
Out
from
the
Womb

The man named his wife Eve (meaning "The life-giving one"), for he said, "She shall become the mother of all mankind" (Gen. 3:20 TLB).

MUCH AS OUR MODERN, sophisticated sensibilities might prefer it otherwise, every person's flesh-and-blood life begins in a very particular place—indeed, in a very particular *person*, who influences much of what takes place thereafter. The first nine months of your life took place in your mother's womb. During that earliest shaping period of your existence, you were a part of your mother's body. What she ate, you ate. What she felt, you felt. Her body, her life, was the limit of yours. In her was life: as long as she lived, you lived; if she died, you died.

The embryonic child *in utero* is so encompassed by the mother that it lacks any natural "memory" of the father's participation in its identity. While studies suggest that a newborn infant may in some sense "recognize" its father, it is not clear whether such recognition is simply a familiarity with the male voice that has been most frequently heard for the previous nine months from outside the mother's womb, or in fact a spiritual bond that accompanies conception. In any case, relationship with the father seems from the outset of our human life intangible, remote, and tenuous.

But while it once was assumed that emotional and spiritual life "began" only after birth itself, the overwhelming evidence of modern research indicates that the unborn child is profoundly affected by and responds both physically and emotionally to a variety of stimuli—from the mother's eating habits and emotional state to music played in her presence.[1] Biblical faith confirms this in recording that John the Baptist stirred within his mother Elizabeth's womb when Mary, pregnant with Jesus, first approached:

> When Elizabeth heard Mary's greeting, the baby moved within her. Elizabeth was filled with the Holy Spirit and said in a loud voice, "You are the most blessed of all women . . . for as soon as I heard your greeting, the baby within me jumped with gladness . . ." (Luke 1:41–44).

If John, or any other child in the womb, can stir with happy feeling, certainly it can also stir with sadness, fear, or any other emotion. Indeed, as John recognized Jesus even when both were in the womb, human life *in utero* recognizes and responds to spiritual reality, even spiritual relationships—such as that of child and father.

This profound biological dependence upon the mother has equally profound implications for the male child's later relationships with women. Certainly, the first woman a male ever loves is his mother, and that love relationship is based upon the most elementary, physical dependence.

Any man who fails to recognize and accept this given fact of his life risks projecting that dependence—and its associated fears—onto the woman he loves later as an adult.

One dramatic example of this phenomenon—so common in popular love songs and courting lore that it is rarely recognized as such—was revealed to me in praying with Dick, who came to me distraught when Renee "rejected" his diligent efforts to "show my love for her." Renee had indicated genuine affection and caring for Dick, but her apparent low self-esteem caused her to become nervous and even angry when he offered flowers, compliments, or his own gestures of affection. "I can tell she wants my love," he declared, clenching his fist in frustration, "but she runs like a scared rabbit whenever I offer it to her!"

The week before, Dick had in desperation left on her car window a note saying, "Without you, life makes no sense." But to his consternation, she was "cold and distant" when they bumped into each other several days later at a company meeting.

At the outset, I explained to Dick that his note translates to a woman, "You are responsible for my life." Indeed, he was attributing saving power to Renee, and, thus making her out to be God. "It's true," Dick eventually confessed. "I really have felt like I couldn't live without her."

When we prayed for understanding and healing, a question came to my mind for Dick: "When in your life were you in fact utterly dependent upon a woman for life, to the point that if she died, you would die yourself?"

Dick knit his brow. "I guess," he said finally, "when I was in my mother's womb."

We then talked for some time about the profound dependency bond between mother and son, and eventually, about Dick and his own mother. When we prayed further, asking the Holy Spirit for help, I had a distinct sense of Dick's mother when she was carrying him—her first child—and a deep fear in her over whether she in fact wanted the child and could handle the responsibilities of motherhood.

"That could very well be," Dick confirmed. "Mom said that Dad was away from home a lot on business when she was pregnant, and I do remember her as always being afraid she couldn't do anything very well."

I then lay my hand on Dick's shoulder and invited him to renounce the bonds of false dependency, and as he did so, I asked Jesus to heal his insecurity from its roots in his mother's womb.

"I know I really do love Renee and want to be with her," Dick said later. "But I know now that my life depends on the

Lord, not on her, and I've got to start getting closer to Him and
let Him start directing my life." Indeed, Dick had begun to see
Renee more accurately. "I realize now that she's been wounded a
lot from her childhood and has her own problems to deal with,
even though she doesn't seem willing to face that. Maybe when
she sees me facing myself like I'm doing now, and getting to the
roots of my problems, she'll want to do that herself. . . ."

Dick sighed. "But maybe not. . . . I guess all I can do now
is turn her over to the Lord and pray for her."

"Just like you're turning yourself over to Him," I added.

The most graphic reflection of this dependence was portrayed
for me in Harry, who at thirty-five had felt worthless and alienated
from others "all my life," especially around women. He feared his
wife's rejection terribly, and she took advantage of this by threatening to leave him whenever she wanted her own way. And then one
day his older sister, whom he saw perhaps once a year, mentioned
off-hand about "the time Mom was going to abort you."

"That really shook me up, to know that," Harry said, shaking even then. He paused. "Do you think that could be where my
fear of women began?"

I suggested we pray and ask the Holy Spirit about it. Before
long, Harry was weeping under the weight of his mother's apparent rejection of him, crying out, "What did I do to make you want
to kill me, Mom?" As we continued to pray, Harry sensed his
mother's fear: she had conceived him during World War II, when
his father was about to leave for battle, and the marriage was
falling apart. In his mind's eye, he "saw" his mother distraught
and asking him to forgive her: "I was so upset and afraid, I didn't
know what to do!" he saw her saying.

"Oh, Mom, I forgive you!" Harry said—with conviction.

We then talked about the experience, and Harry realized
how closely he had felt bound to his mother, how possessive she
had been of him. In telling him about the intended abortion, his
sister had said that his mother was just about to take the prepara-
tory medicine and then threw it into the trash. I suggested we
hold that memory and invite the Lord into it.

"Mom has something in her hand, like she's about to put it in her mouth," Harry said as we began. "But as she goes to do it, Jesus reaches out His hand and stops her. It's like His hand merges into hers, and they throw it into the trash."

I then asked Harry if Jesus had his full permission to say or do all that He wanted in this scene, and Harry nodded. "Yes, Lord, I want all the healing You can give me!"

Almost immediately, he sat up, a look of intensity and amazement on his face. "Jesus is talking to me," he said. "He says, 'All your life you've thought you belonged to your mother, that she saved your life, so you owe your life to her. And so you've tried to please her in all things.

"'But is was not your mother who saved your life. It was I who stayed her hand. It was I who saved you, it is I who am your Lord and Savior. You belong to Me, not to your mother.'"

For several minutes, Harry sat speechless, letting these words and their profound implications for his life sink in. "It's true," he finally said. "I've been afraid of my mother and tried to please her all my life—as if my life belonged to her, as if . . . she'd kill me if I didn't please her. That must be why I get those horrible shakes and shivers whenever my wife threatens to leave me, like it would kill me or something, and why I'm always trying so desperately to please her!"

Harry had much inner work to do afterward in order to approach his wife from a position of manly strength, but these insights allowed him at last to offer himself to the Lord to wean him from fear of his mother into victorious life as a man of God.

Meanwhile, however, the world continues to enforce the male instinct that projects this primal maternal dependency upon the woman loved. "Can't live without you, Baby!" stated variously, is orthodox among pop song writers and listeners. Indeed, the notion has become so customary that a love partner, such as Dick, actually believes that to say this to the woman is a demonstration of love, rather than an infantile abdication of one's life, and thus, pure idolatry.

From this perspective, one wonders about the intent of the Adam and Eve account, in which the man names the woman

"The Life-Giving One." Surely, idolatry lurks here, and it would seem no coincidence that shortly thereafter the man disobeys God in deference to the woman's desires.

Both male and female spiritual development proceeds all too naturally upon this primary and universal assumption of human flesh: "Vitality comes from the woman." This creed is as real and self-evident to human nature as the umbilical cord is to the fetus. Biblical faith, on the other hand, points to a different Source of vitality as the natural role of the mother is superseded by the supernatural role of the Father God.

Thus when Nicodemus sought to discern the source of Jesus' identity and power, Jesus declared, "I am telling you the truth: no one can see the Kingdom of God unless he is born again" (John 3:3).

His own natural, human-centered view of reality blinds Nicodemus from seeing Jesus' point: "How can a grown man be born again?" Nicodemus asked. "He certainly cannot enter his mother's womb and be born a second time!" (v. 4).

Indeed, he cannot. For the idolatry of the flesh must be broken in order to bring the human creature under the proper "kingdom" or authority of God:

> "I am telling you the truth," replied Jesus, "that no one can enter the Kingdom of God unless he is born of water and the Spirit. A person is born physically of human parents, but he is born spiritually of the Spirit" (John 3:5, 6).

Again, Peter declares, "For through the living and eternal word of God you have been born again as the children of a parent who is immortal, not mortal" (1 Peter 1:23).

Meanwhile, this gospel of the flesh that insists vitality comes from the woman is enforced through generations of daughters who, out of this assumption from their own infancy, assume the role of primary vitality when they become wives and mothers, themselves. Many sons, for their part, readily and naturally abdicate to their wives the major portion of family energy, motivation, and initiative.

A significant indicator of where initiative lies can be seen in answering this question: When danger threatens the family, who responds first? In our modern, industrial society, after the lions and snakes have been killed, the elements of nature have been largely subdued, and material necessities are commonly assured, the greatest danger to the family is not physical, but emotional. And when the family is falling apart from within, nine times out of ten the woman is the one who responds by calling clergy or counselor for help.

Such abdication is reflected in the commonly shared joke about the man who declared, "I make all the big decisions in the family, while my wife makes the little ones. I decide whether we should attack Iran, raise or lower taxes, and negotiate with the Russians or stand firm. She decides where we live, how many children we have, where they go to school, who our friends will be, where we go on vacation, and how to spend our money."

Or consider the popular bumper sticker:

God created man and rested; God created woman and nobody's rested since.

And this advice from the old man to the boy in Robert Ruark's *The Old Man and the Boy*:

One thing you will learn . . . is that you must never be lazy in front of anybody. Energetic people get mad at you if you take it easy in front of them. That's one of the troubles with women. They got a dynamo in them, and they run on energy. It pure riles a woman to see a man having any fun that doesn't involve work. That's why fishing was invented, really. It takes you away from the view of industrious people.[2]

We must not submit blindly to easy definitions by branding such jokes and stories as categorically "sexist." Instead, we must dare to ask, is there some objective reality to which they point, some prior and primal perception of the woman as initiator of vitality?

I have ministered to many women crying out to God to deliver them from their fearful compulsion to control others—longing, rather, to rest in faith. Could such a compulsion originate in the daughter's primal sense of the mother as source of life, and subsequent desire to identify with her? Serving as primary vitality for others is an exhausting role, which destroys not only oneself, but others as well. I have observed freedom and healing for such women only insofar as they have been willing to yield to Jesus, confess their attempts to arrogate His power over others, and seek the patience to await His initiative in their lives.

For our own part, we men may well fear the woman's initiative because it reminds us of our own lack of it. In fact, the degree to which a man fears the woman's initiative may be a primary indicator of the extent to which he has not offered himself to Jesus and sought the Father God's initiative. This, of course, requires letting go of the mother/woman as source of life.

All goddess-focused religions ultimately betray roots in such idolatry of the mother/woman and proceed upon natural, earthbound theologies. Thus, they cannot portray true spirituality, which requires a breaking of the powers of the flesh. The natural inclination to attribute ultimate life to the mother/woman simply must be overcome by a supernatural power which is not wholly comprised of the feminine. This is why the Creator God, while encompassing the female, must nevertheless project a male persona. The Genesis account of creation reflects this: "So God created human beings, making them to be like Himself. He created them male and female . . ." (italics mine) (1:27).

This may be interpreted to imply male dominance only as far as the masculine God is required as a counterpoint to break our natural, idolatrous dependence upon the mother/woman.

Beyond the basic fact of initial physical dependence upon the mother, the quality of that bonding experience may also influence the son's later relationships with women. If the boy's maternal bond was painful (perhaps his mother did not want to conceive and thus rejected him) or inappropriate (perhaps she was seductive toward him) the boy later may associate physical bonding with a woman with pain and anxiety. He then may become compulsive about sex either as the freewheeling playboy who is incapable of commitment, or the demanding husband who is fearful of the wife's rejection.

Given the biological and emotional intensity of the mother-son bond, only someone whose intrinsic identification with the boy exceeds that of the mother can draw him away into individuality and adult commitment. Clearly, only the father meets such a requirement; not only has his seed determined the boy's existence equally with the mother's egg, but his being male provides the extra identity factor needed to tip the scales.

Classic developmental psychology concedes primary dependency upon the mother in early years. However, as the child begins to expand his sphere of activity into the world outside the home, the father's role becomes more important as the usher or mentor who calls the child out and initiates or empowers him to function productively in that world.

Unfortunately, going to school does not often provide such a context, largely because elementary school is a feminine environment dominated by female authority figures in the classrooms. Sunday schools are, of course, no exception, and often disregard activities which most boys enjoy at home. "If we only had more slingshots and frogs in Sunday schools, we'd have a lot more men in church later," one friend and fellow pastor lamented.

When a boy reaches puberty, filled with the powerful physical stirrings of his emerging manhood, the father's role becomes critical. If the boy at this point is not called out and away from the mother by the father, those stirrings are overtaken by his natural physical bond with the mother, becoming bound up in her and thus unavailable later to the woman he might love.

A friend of mine discovered this fatherly role on a recent family car trip with his daughter, fifteen, and sons, twelve and seven. One evening he was driving along peacefully while the others slept and suddenly his sleeping twelve-year-old son sat up and cried out, "No, Dad!" Surprised, he turned to see a "heated intensity" in his son's eyes which "perplexed" him. Assuming the boy simply had a nightmare, he reassured him and drove on.

Later the next afternoon, when all were awake and riding

along, he casually asked his son about his outburst the night before. "I had a sex dream," the boy whispered. Startled, my friend sat up quickly—as did the others. "She was naked, and Dad . . . you were standing, watching with me!" As his father sat speechless behind the steering wheel, he added, "And she was Mom. . . ."

Embarrassed, my friend managed some kind words about his son's openness to share so honestly, and drove on.

With remarkable clarity, this boy's dream frames the archetypal beckoning into manhood, which recognizes his physical bond to the mother, and his fear of that, while pleading for the father to shepherd him through and beyond it. Later, I encouraged my friend to record his reflections on the event, and he wrote:

> Some months have passed and life is on its school-days routine, but as a father I am aware that for two of us, life has changed. My son is entering my world; not with a burst of macho, but carefully counting the safety of his steps. Physical changes are signals for the changes in feelings and relationships he is seeing evolve. I am still mindful of the fact that I appeared in his dream. Increasingly, I have sensed his inner petitions for my help in opening the door that stands ajar to a new, exciting, occasionally frightening male self-regard.

Such powerful mysteries of male sexuality are reflected in the very act of physical union. During intercourse, the man physically enters the woman's womb with his male-defining organ. In an emotional/spiritual sense, he is reentering the womb of his infancy—and thus reencountering all the primal *in utero* fears of life-or-death dependency. As therapist Paul Olsen declares in his book, *Sons and Mothers*:

> What a man is frightened of, more than anything else in the vast possibilities of living experience, is dependency, regression to a state in which he becomes an infant in the care of his mother—a mother later unconsciously symbolized by almost all women with whom he comes in contact.[3]

Only one who fears death is compelled to seek and face it continually in order to reassure himself he has power over it. Hence, the "daredevil" model of apparent male courage and the playboy or demanding husband, who must constantly reenter the womb—and more importantly, leave it—to prove he now has power to break the mother's confines.

Searching our modern culture for any popular recognition of the infant-dependency fear during sexual intercourse, I was surprised to find it portrayed in a Willie Nelson song titled, "If You Could Touch Her At All." The singer laments his not having sex more often, but agrees to the woman's once-a-week availability because he's "just flesh and bone." He then declares that the woman "can own any man" through the sex act, during which she holds "his soul in her hand," and after which he is rendered "weak . . . as a newborn child."

Nelson's popularity notwithstanding, Christian men must begin to challenge such idolatry by proclaiming that a woman can "own" only the man who has not allowed the Living God to encounter him—who denies his spiritual nature and sees himself only as flesh-and-bone. The man who has surrendered his life to Jesus belongs to the Father God alone, and thus, cannot be owned by the woman—nor by any other human.

Certainly, the biological/emotional bond between mother and son is a two-way street, and the mother will resist the father's efforts—perhaps even angrily—to take the boy from her. The father who fears the woman's resistance and anger will give up and abandon the boy to her, thereby depriving the boy of identification with manliness, of belonging among men. When the boy later grows up and loves a woman, he cannot offer her the masculine polarity which both he and she need in order to see themselves truthfully and thus help each other to grow. Nor can he call his own son out.

In a powerful and creative insight, poet Robert Bly finds this process of male development portrayed clearly in the Grimm brothers' fairy tale, "Iron Hans," in which a fierce, hairy old man lives at the bottom of a forest lake and jumps out to seize men as they walk by. In the story, Iron Hans—whom Bly calls "the wild-man" inherent to all males—is eventually captured by the king's men and brought into the village square to be displayed in a cage. Hence, society's fear of the "deep masculine" and desire to sub-due and domesticate it.

One day, the king's son is playing with his golden ball—symbolizing, as Bly notes, the perfection or innocence of youth—and it rolls into the wildman's cage. The boy demands it back, but Iron Hans refuses, unless the boy lets him out of the cage. The boy balks, fearing his punishment for doing so, then confesses that he doesn't know where the key is anyhow. The wildman, however, knows: "The key to my cage," he declares, "is under your mother's pillow." As Bly's interviewer comments,

> (T)he young male has to take back the power he has given to his mother and get away from the force field of her bed. He must direct his energies away from pleasing Mommy and toward the search for his own instinctive roots.[4]

The boy's initial fear of stealing the key from Mommy, Bly says, reflects our fear of displeasing her, of leaving her. He empha-sizes that the mother herself is unwilling to give the key to her boy, who must seize it himself if he is to break away from her sphere of influence and enter that of Iron Hans:

> If you went up to your mother and said, "I want the key so I can let the wildman out," she'd say, "Oh no, you just get a job," or, "Come over here and give Mommy a kiss." There are very few mothers in the world who would release that key from under the pillow, because they are intuitively aware of what would happen next—namely, they would lose their nice boys. The possessiveness that some mothers exercise on sons . . . cannot be overestimated.[5]

And so, in the story, the boy steals the key and lets the wildman out. Fearful of what his parents will do to him when they find out, he goes with the wildman back into the forest. Bly speculates upon a different scenario:

The wildman could go back to his pond, so that the split happens over again; by the time the parents come back, the wildman is gone and the boy has replaced the key. He could become a corporate executive, an ordained minister, a professor. He might be a typical twentieth-century male.[6]

Significantly, in the story the boy stays in the forest until years later, when a nearby kingdom is threatened; properly trained by Iron Hans, he returns and overcomes the foe—and marries the king's daughter. The story is clear: in order to exercise saving manly power in the world and bond with a woman, a man must have separated from his mother and bonded with the masculine one who is greater even than his own father.

Where in our modern culture can we find such a male need affirmed? I have sought model stories which might portray a father and/or group of men who "call out" the boy away from the mother. Yet, while some hint at the boy's longing for that, few offer it. Huckleberry Finn, Holden Caufield of *Catcher in the Rye*, Luke Skywalker of *Star Wars*, Johnny Cash's "A Boy Named Sue"—all proceed from the father's apparent absence. Certainly, Faulkner's short story, "The Bear," which portrays the boy's slaying of the beast among the men and being smeared with its blood, qualifies.

A more accessible story, however, was related by Garrison Keillor in one of his *Prairie Home Companion* monologues. When he was fourteen, during ice fishing season in Minnesota, his uncle and several other men came to his house after dark and invited him to go with them to a hut out on the frozen lake for a night's fishing together. Keillor recalls the mystery in hearing "guys laughing out there in the dark, out on the lake," and knowing that such places were "where guys go to be with other guys, to get away from women."

There, Keillor discovered, the men did indeed talk about "things you couldn't talk about back at the house" around women. "Out at the ice house," in fact,

. . . guys could go out there and just let it fly; you could be loose and tell lies and chew and spit when you wanted to. And when the mood would seize you, you could go out and take a leak out back in the snow. . . . I remember going out there with the others. It was a moment of brotherhood for a boy, a boy filled with all those doubts and fears. . . .[7]

Having thus surveyed my own culture as one drawn to a deeper sense of my own masculinity, I find such offerings helpful, but ultimately unsatisfying. After some reflection, I have realized why: though they hint at mystery, none explicitly proclaims the essential spiritual dimension of manhood. As with virtually all enterprises in our Western-scientific culture, I eventually feel abandoned at the authentic essence of my being. However creative and insightful we are in our attempts to invoke manhood we remain captives of our proud naturalistic mind set, and thus are utterly incapable of addressing ultimate, spiritual reality. Even as our masculine spirits cry out for connection to our spiritual Creator, our rational, human-centered culture will not tolerate the presence of the Father God, much less submit to His call.

The Western Church, for its part, offers little help. If it has not become secularized, it has surely become femininized—as we shall see in a later chapter—and thus, in either sense, incapable of ministering to this profound need among men. To find an appropriate starting point in our quest for a model of male affirmation that is self-consciously social and spiritual, we must go to other, Third-World cultures. There, we shall find that societies which we Western males have long regarded as "primitive" are in fact far more advanced than we are in recognizing and meeting this basic need in the boy to be "called out," and thus validated by men.

3

Come Out, Son of Our People!

EARLY IN THE FALL of 1964, at the adventurous, indestructible age of twenty, I received an invitation from the U.S. Peace Corps to teach mathematics at a boys' high school in Nigeria. Equipped with my bachelor's degree in that subject, including a minor in physics, I had soon set out for the "Dark Continent," asking not what my country could do for me, but how I could share the boons of Western civilization with other, apparently less fortunate people.

After several months of teaching young African men about congruent triangles, however, I was startled—and appropriately humbled—by a simple question while chatting with a student about American families.

"How is it in America that a boy is called by the men?" he asked, matter-of-factly.

I hesitated, wondering if perhaps my student were using improper syntax. "What do you mean?"

49

"In your own village in America," he replied, "how did the men come for you, when you were reaching the proper age to come out from your mother's house?"

"Oh," I said readily, smiling graciously, "in America, unlike here in your village, the mother and father both live in the same house, so that sort of thing really isn't necessary."

Clearly puzzled by my response, the young man moved as if to speak, hesitated, and then sat quietly, knitting his brow. Unsure what more to say, I changed the subject.

Fortunately—though I could not appreciate it at the time— I had occasion later to ask a Nigerian teacher to describe for me his own initiation rite as a boy. Like a seed planted in dry ground, his story remained dormant in my mind and heart for perhaps twenty years, until at last I began to soak in the fraternal longings of my fellow men. Today, I treasure it, sharing it as often as possible. When I do, I wish I could contact that student who asked me the question, which I, in my cultural deprivation, simply had no way of understanding at the time.

In the rural village where he lived, the father, who often has several wives, lives by himself in his own hut, while his wives each have their own hut nearby. A boy lives with his mother until he reaches the proper age, usually about eleven. Then, one evening the village elders and the boy's father appear outside the mother's hut, together with a drummer and a man wearing a large mask over his head. The word for "mask" is the same as that for "spirit"; so as the masked man steps out first from among the men both to call the boy out and to usher him from the mother to the men, the spiritual dimension of manhood is understood from the outset as primary and essential.

At the signal of a sharp drumbeat, the mask/spirit approaches the mother's door, dancing and shouting, "Come out! Come out!" After several retreats and then thrusting forth to announce his presence and intention, the mask/spirit rushes the mother's door and beats upon it loudly: *Bam! Bam! Bam!* "Come out! Son of our people, *come out!*"

Eventually—perhaps after two or three such "approaches" by the mask/spirit—the mother opens the door tentatively, shielding her son behind her. At this, the elders and the father join in the chant: "Come out, son of our people, come out!" Significantly, the mask/spirit does not enter the mother's hut to seize the boy, but rather, waits for him to step out on his own from behind his mother.

Louder the elders chant, sharper the drum beats sound, more feverishly the mask/spirit dances, and more firmly the mother protests—until finally, she steps aside.

It is the moment of truth for every boy in the village.

Standing there before the threshold of his mother's house, he hesitates. Beside and behind him holds all that is tender and reassuring and known and secure. Before him, and within him, cries out all that is mysterious and sharp and powerful and true.

"*Come out!*" the men shout.

Hesitantly, wanting but not daring to look at his mother, the boy steps forth from the dark womb of his mother's hut into the outside—born again, this time as a child of the father.

At once the mask/spirit seizes his wrist and rushes him over to the father and elders—lest in his fear he have second thoughts—where he is joined with the other boys called out for that year's initiation. Behind him, a wail of mourning breaks forth from his mother; the men around him burst into a victory shout. The drummer picks up the sharp and decisive beat, and the group moves on to the next boy's hut.

Once gathered, the group of boys is led out of the village to a special place in the forest, where they are instructed for the next two weeks. Manly skills from thatch roof construction to hunting are taught first. Then the boy enters a period of fasting for several days, thus turning his focus from physical satisfaction to spiritual discipline. During this time, the boy is circumcised and, while he is healing, taught clan history. Circumcision, of course, is a symbolic cutting of the penis, that is, a yielding of manhood to the power in whose name the cut is demanded—in this case, the clan. The physical pain of the operation would seem to connect the boy graphically with the sufferings of the men in his tribal heritage.

Meanwhile, back in the village, the father builds his son a

small hut of his own. Upon returning from the wilderness ordeal, the boy is regarded as a young man; when he enters the village, his mother is not permitted to greet him. He proceeds directly to his own new house, separate from his mother's; that evening, he receives from his father a gun, a piece of farmland, and a hoe—his stake with which to establish his manhood in the clan.

Hearing this story at twenty, as a world traveler romantically "on my own," I scoffed. Today, at forty-three, I weep. For I have grown strong enough to face what I and my fellow twentieth-century Western males have lost. The pounding on your mother's door, the cry of the man-affirming spirit to "Come out!," the chorus of older men waiting to receive you, the father's gift of accoutrements—all these tap deep, deep longings within me that words cannot express.

Hearing such a story, I am humbled, emptied—no, revealed as empty.

What does my own culture offer as a validation of manhood? The driver's license at sixteen; and freedom at eighteen to join the Army, attend pornographic movies, and to buy cigarettes and beer. The message is clear: becoming a man means operating a powerful machine, killing other men, masturbating, destroying your lungs, and getting drunk.

We are lost males, all of us: cast adrift from the community of men, cut off from our masculine heritage—abandoned to machines, organizations, fantasies, drugs.

I realize the depth of our predicament when I describe this African male initiation rite to groups, for the most frequent question afterward is, "Does the mother *really* hold the boy behind her when the mask/spirit approaches her hut, and cry when the mask/spirit seizes him? Or isn't she just playacting, going along with the game, so to speak?"

I have come to regard such a question as kin to the unspoken attitude of Western Christians before the Eucharist: Does anything really happen to people who take the bread and wine? Or isn't the congregation just playacting, going along, as it were, with the game which the church insists on perpetuating?

God help us when we have so forgotten who we are, and so

lost our experience of the event which brought us into being, that we wander in such spiritual amnesia.

Gently, I explain that yes, the drama of the initiation rite anticipates a certain response from the mother. But in doing so, the rite does not define that response, but authenticates it. In fact, no mother who has enjoyed the devotion of her son can readily give it up. The release and proper growth of the boy require a community-ordained ritual to which her natural, self-centered impulses must yield.

The ritual, through the spirit who initiates and presides over it, allows the individual mother both to express her genuine pain and to submit at last to the larger authority of the spirit—thus yielding to the boy's new emotional/spiritual "birth" even as years earlier she yielded the baby in labor, itself.

Clearly, without such a ritual, the mother is not likely to be confronted with this, her essential role—and her natural, self-centered desires for the boy then prevail over his life, even into adulthood. In a convoluted myopia, the boy in later physical maturity cannot look beyond the woman to find manhood, and therefore seeks it in women, through sexual relationships. If his manhood has never been confirmed by identifying with the larger community of men through his father, he constantly seeks it with woman after woman, remaining forever "invalid" in his manhood.

In the face of such realizations, I am overwhelmed. How in the world—indeed, how in *our* world—can we Western men begin to rediscover this basic male need and meet it? If in fact the father is the key to a boy's crossing the threshold into manhood, what can those do who had no father, or perhaps whose father did not appropriately call him out from his mother?

Certainly, a seed of hope may be found in the fact that the origin of manhood cannot lie in the father alone, but only in some greater masculine Source from which the father himself must draw. The father becomes the sole focus of manhood only in a society such as our own, which lacks bonds of male "tribal" fellowship—not in societies such as the Nigerian village, where the boy's father appears before the mother's hut as part of a larger group of men, who themselves stand in the background, behind the mask/spirit.

A man must beware the temptation to skirt the pain of being cut off from his father; to do so is to let that pain bind and control him from the deeper unconscious to which he banishes it. He must start where he genuinely is, however painful, if he is to get where he needs to go.

At the same time, he must beware the companion temptation to judge and condemn his father for what the latter did not give him. The man who confesses his pain by bringing it to Jesus at the cross will begin to see that his father was not called out by his own father, so didn't know how to call out his son. One's father is not the oppressor, but a fellow victim, a brother in mutual need of manly affirmation. When a man allows Jesus to carry his tears for his own loss into tears for his father's loss when the latter was also a boy, he has begun to become a man of God at last.

Weeping for generations of loss, however, cannot by itself make you a man of God. Perhaps more significantly, neither can it save your own son from being so wounded. The communal dimension of manhood, largely discounted by our "modern" society, must be rediscovered and reaffirmed, as must the larger Source of manhood which beckons both fathers and sons. When enough men have begun to face and cry out their longing for manly affirmation, the time comes to act. The man who would move through and beyond his individual pain into an authentic, viable manhood today, must acknowledge and connect with the deeper masculine Source which calls a man out—even from his father—to fulfill his unique, individual calling.

The Christian man may trust that such a transcendent manhood is rooted in the Father God who created all men and beckons him through Jesus.

And so at last, I wonder: what might an authentic Christian male initiation look like? Surely, it must be termed a sacrament, namely, the outward and visible sign of the inward and spiritual grace of godly manhood.

I think of our modern church and shudder at the task. So many, many women—two-thirds of all church members, according to a recent survey, and as any pastor knows, an even greater portion of active members. Dare I begin such a portrait?

Dare I not?

For I feel the longing in myself, and in so many men I have prayed with—and know that I must forge ahead. To turn back is to run from the lion.

And so I pray: Help us, Lord. We're tired of slavery, frightened of the desert, yet longing for the Promised Land. Lead us with Your vision.

I imagine: One evening after dinner, Dad gets up, mentioning casually that he's going out to the store for a few minutes. Outside, he drives to the church, where he is met by the male elders and the other fathers of boys to be initiated. The men gather in the sanctuary to worship and rededicate their own manhood to God, praying that together they might be a fitting channel for God's spirit of manhood to each boy. All lay hands on each father, one at a time, and pray for God's strength and wisdom to fill him for guiding his son. For boys who have no father available, godly men are appointed as surrogates.

All the men then drive to the first boy's house—perhaps in one or two vans—and while a male pastor approaches the door, the men stand on the front lawn singing hymns.

The doorbell rings. The mother opens the door:

Faith of our fathers, living still . . .

Surprised to see the pastor and the men outside singing, she stands there, uncertain.

"We've come for Dan," the pastor says.

In spite of dungeon, fire and sword . . .

"But . . . but what for?" she asks. "I didn't know there was a youth group event tonight . . . ?"

O how our hearts beat high with joy
When e'er we hear that glorious word!

"This is not for the youth group," the pastor explains, "this is for the men."

Faith of our fathers, holy faith!
We will be true to thee till death.

"Well, I . . . I don't know," the mother says, glancing uneasily at the men singing out front. "Actually, Danny's father's not home just now, so you'll have to wait until. . . ."

"What's all that singing outside?" the boy calls out from the living room. "What's going on?" He comes to the door, beside his mother.

Rise up, O men of God! Have done with lesser things . . .

Seeing the men out front, the boy draws up, tense.

"We want you to come with us tonight, Dan," the pastor tells him.

Give heart and mind and soul and strength
To serve the King of kings!

"Dan!" his father calls out from the group.

"What's your father doing out there with those men?" the mother exclaims.

"Dad!" the boy calls back—still uneasy, but encouraged to see his father there.

Lift high the cross of Christ!
Tread where His feet have trod . . .

"Come on out, Dan!" his father shouts. "Come out with us!"

As brothers of the Son of man, rise up, O men of God!

The boy looks up at the minister, who nods—and waits. "But it's cold outside," the mother protests. "And Danny hasn't finished his dessert. . . ."

Stand up, stand up for Jesus, the trumpet call obey . . .

"I appreciate your concern," the pastor says, then turning to the boy, "You can go and get your coat. Your dad has already put together the clothes you'll be needing."

The boy hesitates, licking a trace of apple pie from his lips.

Forth to the mighty conflict, in this his glorious day . . .

"Come on, Dan!" his father shouts. "Let's go!"

Ye that are men now serve him against unnumbered foes
Let courage rise with danger, and strength to strength oppose.

A pause . . . then all at once, the boy spins on his heels and dashes to his bedroom, comes running back grasping his coat. As he steps out the front door, the pastor nods graciously to the mother and puts an arm around him. The two head out onto the lawn as a mighty chorus arises:

A mighty fortress is our God! A bulwark never failing;
Our helper He amid the flood of mortal ills prevailing.
For still our ancient foe doth seek to work us woe;
His craft and power are great, and armed with cruel hate,
On earth is not his equal.

Did we in our own strength confide, our striving would be
  losing,
Were not the right man on our side, the one of God's own
  choosing;
Dost ask who that may be? Christ Jesus, it is he:
Lord Sabaoth his name, from age to age the same,
And he must win the battle.

When all the boys have been gathered this way, they are driven to a church campground for a period of discipline and instruction. This would include:

- An opening worship in which each boy is taught to memorize Romans 12:1 and 2, offering himself to God's service and opening himself to let God transform him inwardly during the initiation period
- Time to remember the men from whom the boy comes: stories of his father and grandfather, stories of American history
- Time to remember the God from whom all men come: Bible stories and biblical standards of behavior
- Learning to pray, both alone and with others
- A time of fasting during which the boy is taught its biblical basis and purpose
- Teaching the nature of sexuality and how to relate to women with both compassion and strength
- Aptitude testing for professional skills, followed by a general session in which the men sit as a panel and share frankly about their jobs, inviting questions afterward
- Rigorous physical exercise
- Daily individual prayer, Bible reading, and journal-keeping
- Prayer and counseling for each boy to heal inner emotional wounds
- Talks by much older, godly men about what life was like when they were boys, and what their faith has meant to them
- A closing worship in which the men call each boy forward, lay hands upon him, and pray for him to receive the Holy Spirit as in the traditional rite of confirmation.

Clearly, all this requires considerable planning and organization—the sort of gifts which most churches rely upon women to exercise. To make such a commitment, the adult men of the church must of course be convinced of its necessity. That is, they must have dared to face their own need to be affirmed as men, their own emptiness and longing for that out of their own boyhood. For the witness of the cross is that human brokenness offered up to God mediates His transforming, resurrecting power.

May the men of our churches become so boldly humble that their sons are empowered to serve God mightily as the men of tomorrow's Church.

4
She
Left
Me!

ABOVE ALL, JOHN WAS a nice guy. His ready smile, helpful attitude, and seemingly unconditional acceptance of others made him easy to like.

When Susan left him, he was crushed.

An intelligent, ambitious young woman, she had worked her way up from the waitress job she held when they met to being manager in a large advertising firm. Having known both during the five years they were together, I had often sensed a root problem in the relationship; after the shock of the split had worn off, and I had offered John my support and comfort, the appropriate opportunity arose for me to express it.

"I just don't understand it," he sighed one day, shaking his head sadly. "We were together so long. I just assumed we'd always be together."

I hesitated. "John . . . ," I began, "what did you and Susan fight about?"

John drew up quickly, a puzzled look on his face. "What do you mean?"

"I just mean, how did you guys handle your differences?"

His eyes lowered. "Actually, I guess we didn't really fight much at all. Hardly ever, in fact, in all those years."

Gently, I proceeded. "I know Susan is a beautiful person. But I also happen to know she's no saint, and has her rough edges like all of us. How did you handle it, say, when she'd fly off the handle once in a while? I mean, did you get angry at her at all?"

John sat quietly for several moments. "I guess . . . I never did get angry at her."

"You mean she never did anything that made you feel angry?"

Another silence, longer this time. "Well, I can't say I never *felt* angry at her . . . ; I guess I just never expressed it."

I did what I had to do. "Why not?" I asked.

John looked away, then dropped his head. "I guess . . . I was afraid of losing her."

Feeling his pain, I hesitated. This must be like a surgeon feels, I thought, knowing the emotional incision had to be made. "And what happened?" I said.

John sighed deeply. "I lost her."

Recalling that scene today, years later, I am torn: I recognize my own reluctance then to wield the "sword of truth" in behalf of my friend, and I wish I had been able to do so earlier, when John and Susan were still going together. But would he have been able to hear it then? No matter; today I regard it as a friend's responsibility. Slowly, steadily, we men are learning the sharper dimension of caring and love for others.

Nevertheless, I believe that John's reaction to Susan is a paradigm for men in our time. The women's liberation movement of the 1960s proclaimed that we men were free at last to be more gentle and hence, to develop our more "feminine" side—even as women were free to be more bold and, in that traditional sense, more "masculine." Twenty years later, however, the pendulum has today reached its apogee, and we men are scrambling to recover our manly strength, while the women themselves are crying out for us to do so. As Susan told me later,

> I know it sounds crazy to say this, but I wish John could've been angry—just once in awhile—so I wouldn't have felt guilty, as if I were the only mean one in the relationship when I'd fly off the handle occasionally. I realize he was afraid to lose me, and that made me feel all the more guilty when I'd think about leaving. I guess I just got tired of being the spark plug, the only one with any energy, direction, or plans.

Poet Robert Bly has aptly portrayed this phenomenon as the "soft male":

> They're lovely, valuable people—I like them—and they're not interested in harming the earth or starting wars or working for corporations. There's something favorable toward life in their whole general mood and style of living.
> But something's wrong. Many of these men are unhappy: there's not much energy in them. They are life-preserving but not exactly *life-giving*. And why is it you often see these men with strong women who positively radiate energy? Here we have a finely tuned young man, ecologically superior to his father, sympathetic to the whole harmony of the universe, yet he himself has no energy to offer.[1]

In developing our sensitive, "feminine" side, we men today have "learned to be receptive," yet still lack an essential male ingredient in relating to women:

> In every relationship something fierce is needed once in awhile: both the man and the woman need to have it. He was nurturing, but something else was required—for the relationship, for his life. The male was able to say, "I can feel your pain and I consider your life as important as mine, and I will take care of you and comfort you." But he could not say what *he* wanted and stick by it; that was a different matter.[2]

Perhaps not surprisingly, Bly's final diagnosis draws upon the sword image:

> In *The Odyssey,* Hermes instructs Odysseus, when he is approaching a kind of matriarchal figure, that he is to lift, or show Circe, his sword. It (is) difficult for many of the younger males (today) to distinguish between showing the sword and hurting someone. . . . They (have) learned so well not to hurt anyone that they (can't) lift the sword, even to catch the light of the sun on it! Showing a sword doesn't mean fighting: there's something joyful in it.[3]

From his wholly secular position, Bly cannot recognize the "sword of the Spirit," which bears God's healing truth even as it cuts through our fleshly pride and pretensions. Yet he has grasped well the basic fear among us men today that to "lift the sword" can only be destructive. At the root of this fear lies a narrow view of pain, an unwillingness to recognize that pain is essential to growth, as to life itself. Every woman who has borne a child knows this from the pain of labor. Our Christian faith proclaims it through the Cross; there is no resurrection to new life without suffering death of the self.

Certainly, no sane person enjoys hurting another. But we must be willing to risk hurting one another as well as being hurt, if we are to bear life to our relationships. A surgeon, for example, is not a knife-wielding thief. In fact, what surgeons do intentionally causes pain—and we pay them to do it, because we all agree that the immediate pain of the operation is preferable to the long-range pain of continued illness.

At its most basic level, lifting the sword of truth can simply enforce a merciful economy of pain, as one would tear off the bandage quickly, rather than "gently" pulling—one hair at a time. Certainly, the truth can be wielded as a weapon of destruction; but Christians are bound by the biblical standard in which relationships are strengthened under Christ "by speaking the truth in a spirit of love" (Eph. 4:15). We may fear lifting the sword of truth, because we do not genuinely love the other person.

Years ago, a friend of mine with a master's degree in litera-
ture and a deep commitment to "social justice for the poor,"
married an uneducated woman far below his social class, who was
fervently devoted to him. After much inner frustration and struggle, he came to see his dishonesty, that he "just wanted to rebel
against my parents and show everyone else how righteous I was in
'caring for the poor.'" Eventually, he initiated a divorce. "I wish
I'd had the courage to be honest with myself from the beginning
of the relationship, and cut things off way back then," he declared
to me afterward. "But I kept telling myself how badly that would
hurt her." Shaking his head in dismay, he added, "Never marry
someone to do her a favor."

In generations past, the fear of pain was commonly associated with women, who might, for example, faint at the sight of
blood. A man, on the other hand, was expected to be able to endure pain, and in that sense, to acknowledge its necessity. The fact
that men today are more likely to balk at pain may well suggest a
disproportionate feminine influence in our upbringing.

Indeed, my friend John—like many young men today—had
been raised by his mother since age eight, when his parents divorced. His father had not been around to teach him how to lift
the sword as a man; in fact, John's brief stories from memory
suggested that his father was unable to do so himself. Susan,
meanwhile, was one of the strong, energetic women of whom Bly
speaks, never at a loss for an agenda of her own. John simply had
no inner father-man voice to encourage him at times even to say,
"Susan, I insist that we do things my way 50 percent of the time"
or, "Enough of your griping! If you're willing to sit down and
work this out together, let's do it; if not, let me know when
you're ready and we'll talk about it, but until then I have better
things to do than stand and listen to ugliness from the woman I
love." But John could not present a credible threat either to insist
on equitability or to leave and trust her to come to respect him in
her own time. And so he lost her.

In his book, *Passive Men, Wild Women,* Pierre Mornell notes
that a man's giving in to his wife's agenda "may only serve to
compound the problem by having the wife's demands increase":

Personally, I think when such a wife keeps goading her husband it's because, unconsciously, she is actually threatened by the control she is developing over him. The control and power to get him to behave as she wants. The husband's repeatedly giving in to her is further evidence that he is indeed a passive and easily manipulated man. . . .

In a sense the wife provokes her husband, and she may constantly provoke him, to test his limits and to test his ability to remain himself.[4]

Certainly, such provocation may often lead to a fight. But the man who understands the healing power in the sword need not shrink away. As Mornell declares,

But the fact is that although sometimes destructive, (these arguments) can also serve a constructive purpose in this kind of marriage.

The inevitable fight not only releases tension, but also forces the husband to state what he thinks and how he feels. It involves him with his wife at a feeling level. Like good sex, a good argument means that a husband is finally active, involved and engaged with his wife. It is tangible proof that he can be strong. In the midst of battle, he is no longer a wet noodle.[5]

"Sometimes my wife wants to fight over the craziest things," as one man exclaimed after I read this to a men's class. "The other day it was over where to hang a picture on the wall. I couldn't care less where it hung, but she kept needling me every time I made a suggestion, even after she asked for my opinion!"

He paused. "Do you think she just wants me to get kind of . . . more involved with her somehow?"

I replied that he might well be correct, and encouraged him simply to ask her.

We men, that is, are more geared for content and solutions than process and relationships; the woman is less concerned with what she's fighting about than with whom she's fighting.

Granted, as Mornell freely admits, the same woman who has urged her man to fight may balk at and even resist his new strength:

Although she wants her husband to take charge and be decisive, she will resist giving up the control to which she has grown accustomed. She will undermine his initial efforts. But, in one sense, her reaction is a test. And if a man is to pass that test, he must fight through her initial line of defense. He must prove that he is not indifferent and apathetic. He must prove that he is strong enough to fight not only for his values, but for his wife.[6]

When I was in high school during the fifties, a popular song titled, "Johnny, Get Angry," featured a female singer's asking her boyfriend to give her "the biggest lecture I've ever had" after her improper behavior. Declaring that she wants "a brave man," the singer indicates in the last line of the chorus what Johnny's daring to get angry really means to her as she pleads, "Johnny, show me that you care, really care, for me."

Years ago as a college freshman, I took boxing as part of the required P.E. program. For sparring practice, we were paired off by weight only, and at one point a fellow student complained that his partner, while the same weight, had much longer arms.

"You've got to work so that you get inside your opponent's reach," the coach declared.

"But he'll batter me!" the student protested.

"Only if you stay outside his reach. Sure, he'll probably catch you a few times when you're coming in, but that's your only chance. If you're willing to take a few shots at first, you'll get inside and whip him."

Engaging an angry woman can be like boxing with someone who has long arms. If you "stay outside," trying to calm her down and backing off or giving in, she'll batter you. But if you're willing to take a few blows, and move deliberately closer to her—perhaps insisting that you sit down and work it out, and refusing to let her harsh words continue to lash you when you love her as you do—both of you can win the match.

Certainly, being able to "take a few punches" and move in closer to the angry woman requires a basic level of emotional health on the man's part. Sadly, many men today bear deep wounds caused by demanding mothers or distant fathers, and in confronting the woman he loves, such a man is ruled either by suppressed hostility toward his mother or the model of withdrawal from his father.

Often, the man who grew up with such parents has seen his mother's anger flare up and ultimately become destructive without a strong father to counter it with manly restraint. He has thus learned to fear the woman's anger, and is anxious to suppress his wife's rage even when it is not directed at him.

Jim and Sally were the classic example of this dynamic when they came to me for help. "My work is a real pressure-cooker," Sally declared, "and when I come home, I'm often angry at somebody I've dealt with during the day. I need somehow to vent that with Jim, but he just gets defensive and shuts me down, as if I were angry at him. Worse, he even takes the side of the person I'm angry at, telling me I should be 'more understanding of others!' That drives me up the wall, until I really *am* angry at him—for not letting me be angry—and soon I'm unloading it all on him and we're both at each other's throats."

Questioning revealed that Jim's parents had argued bitterly and often, stopping only when his father gave in. "I hated to see my father get whipped like that all the time by my mother," Jim declared. "I just wanted to stop the whole thing, especially to get Mom to stop beating up on Dad like that."

When Jim had seen the pattern clearly, we prayed and invited Jesus to come into a scene of the parents' fighting. Without addressing the parents at all, Jesus simply put His arm around Jim, and turned him away from them both. As they disappeared from the scene, Jesus spoke to Jim: "Your mom and dad are responsible for their own problems. It's not your responsibility to stop them from fighting. Let go and give them to Me, and let Me teach you how to love your wife even when she's angry."

At that, Jim confessed that he had indeed taken on a responsibility which was not his to bear, and he released his combative parents to the Lord. He then asked Jesus to guide and teach him how to listen to his wife's anger when necessary, and even when lovingly but firmly to speak a word of restraint to her when necessary.

Often, of course, such a mother has focused her anger on

the boy himself, and the pain of that memory keeps him afraid to speak a firm word of restraint to his wife—which insures that the pattern of husband-whipping continues into yet another generation. In such cases, the man needs to disengage, to pull out of the battle for awhile and go to the Father God for healing.

I had been discussing this phenomenon with a friend when our conversation turned to prayer, and then to the power in praying for physical healing. After exchanging stories of how we had each prayed for healing in others with varying results, my friend remarked that his most successful effort at healing prayer had not been with another human being, but in fact, with his pet canary—much to his surprise.

Noting that he had two birds, a male and a female, in the cage together, he recalled coming home one evening to find the male leaning lethargically against the side of the cage, his head hanging low. Concerned, he was about to open the cage door when the hen darted across the cage and began pecking furiously at the male, who only shifted weakly even when she tore tufts of feathers from his wing. Upon closer inspection, my friend noted from the male's outward appearance that the hen must have been attacking him for some time.

Not knowing what else to do, he took the male from the cage, and sat down, holding it in his hand. He then simply began praying for the bird's healing. After perhaps a half hour, he decided to put the male in a second cage, alone and apart from the hen, and to call the vet in the morning.

When he had placed the bird on the empty cage perch, however, my friend was surprised when, after a moment, it began to chirp, quietly at first, and then loudly, with great gusto.

"He kept on chirping brightly, until I knew that was no sick bird any more," he said. And so he put it back into the original cage.

Together we marveled at this amazing story of God's healing. And then, it occurred to me to ask: "But what happened with the hen?"

"Well, that was amazing, too," he declared. "Not long after I set the male back on the perch, she came right over after him, as she'd apparently been doing all day before I came home. He just sat there as she came over, but when she went ahead and took a peck at him, he flew into a raging screech and charged back at her furiously, pecking at her. He didn't follow her over to the corner and hurt her, but as soon as she flew off away from him, he went back to his position and began preening himself. After that, she never pecked at him again, and they were chirping together before long."

Today, when working with the "hen-pecked" male who is afraid of the woman, I tell this story and ask him, "Where are you personally in this story? Are you sick and weak, allowing the woman to destroy you? Or have you dared to separate yourself from her and place yourself in God's hands for healing—that is, have you responded to the Father God as He calls you out and away from the mother? Or, have you allowed God to heal your wounded masculinity and then reentered the cage, and reengaged the woman with His strength and courage?"

I am quite sure that some men who read this will balk at my use of the bird image, especially younger men who have come of age since the feminist movement began. "It's too physical, too crude," some may say. I have no argument with men who feel this way and are getting along well with themselves and their women. This book is simply not written for such men, but for those in need of healing.

Significantly, canaries are made to chirp and are happiest when they are chirping. The hen canary is not happiest when she's pecking away at her sick male companion. She would rather be singing beside him on the same perch. Yet such harmony is contingent upon the male's willingness to demonstrate strength to her, even—especially—in the face of her anger.

The most honest of women know this, and feminist leaders themselves are proclaiming it, sometimes desperately.

In an article ominously titled, "Wormboys: Is He a Wimp, Or Isn't He?" Deborah Laake laments the proliferation of men who effectively shrink from initiative and responsibility. She defines a "wormboy" through questions to her female readers:

Does your partner avoid confrontation, with you and everyone else? Is he unconcerned with excellence in his work? Is he lazy?[7]

Such traits are revealed most readily, she suggests, when simple decisions need to be made:

Although you both work, when the two of you go to dinner, do you choose the restaurant? If you ask your partner to suggest a place, does he tell you solicitously that he "just isn't sure what you feel like eating"?
  Do you alone comb the entertainment sections of local periodicals for movies, plays, and events? Are you the one who suggests and arranges get-togethers with friends? Do you schedule all your weekends out of town together? Does your partner just "go along"?[8]

Women are beginning to discern a difference between a genuine desire to please them and a fear of responsibility:

A woman in charge of a wormboy's leisure time can start to feel like a real bitch. The situation may have begun with the two of you offering well-meaning suggestions, only some of which were agreed upon. But a wormboy collapses in defeat when a few of his ideas are rejected, and suddenly the responsibility for fun falls to you.[9]

In a very real sense, the woman is simply looking for the masculine energy that expresses itself by taking the initiative:

A friend of mine . . . after a long weekend out of town with a crowd, returned home in the company of a man who took it upon himself to lessen his fellow passengers' boredom. "Let's sing," he would say, and then lead the singing. Or, "Alright, now let's play a game." My friend was very impressed with this level of initiative. . . . A strong woman is capable of a big life with someone, and every time she finds she is not sharing energies with a partner but is actually giving her own energy away, she wonders a little more achingly if she will find companionship *fervent* enough to enlarge living.[10]

Cartoonist Lynda Barry makes the point in a series of frames titled, "The Sensitive Male." Only the male face is visible throughout, and he begins apparently in response to the question of where the two will go out for the evening:

> Man: Tonight? It's up to you, Angel.
> Woman: Why do *I* end up making all of the decisions in this relationship, Bill?
> M: Because I want to treat you equally, Dear. The last thing I want to be is a dominant male, Honey.
> W: I don't have anything to worry about.
> M: I want this relationship to *work*. More wine?
> W: Look, Bill, I realize you are trying to be sensitive to my needs, but do you have to be such a *wimp* about it?
> M: I resent that, my Darling.
> W: OK, Bill, listen. I want *you* to make all of the decisions tonight, all right?
> M: Whatever you say, Dear. But what if I make decisions which oppress you? Or, what if I start being macho by *accident?* What if I *like* it? Are you sure you can handle being confronted with my powerful masculinity, Honey? I mean, maybe you should think this over.[11]

As an antiwar activist and supporter of women's liberation who came of age in the sixties, I read Barry's cartoon and don't know whether to laugh or cry. I have done both. But I have also found myself angry. What indeed, I wonder, do women these days want? First, in the fifties, we were too demanding and overpowering, and they complained; now, we are sensitive and understanding, and they complain. As "wormboy" critic Laake herself admits,

> Ten years ago we were complaining that men all feel this need to perform this macho role and they think they've got to be strong and they can't cry. And now we've released them from that. We wanted to destroy sex roles, so we destroyed them, and now we're complaining.[12]

Even as I write this, I look at my words and am dismayed at how woman-centered they are. My concern focuses on what the woman wants from me, on pleasing her. Idolatry lurks here. As Bly would ask, when does the man say what he wants and stick by it?

Similarly, Laake, even as she admits the confusion wrought by women's attitudes, simply assumes that men have become more sensitive and less macho because women have "released" us to be so, not because we have chosen to exercise such freedom.

To the extent that we men have abdicated initiative to women, Laake and the others cannot be blamed for their presumption. Indeed, she just may be right. If so, that would explain the spurious aspect of our "sensitivity" today.

Whatever sensitivity a man has simply because the woman has released him to have it may make him similar to the woman, but it can never comprise the manly sensitivity which both he and the woman need. A woman can only release a man to feminine sensitivity as defined in the mother—that is, feeling for the other, drawing the other to oneself and nurturing. She cannot release him to masculine sensitivity, as defined in the father—that is, listening for the larger word of truth and lifting its sword in the other's behalf.

In fact, the woman must always draw short of releasing the man to any depth of perception or sensitivity which might threaten her power in the relationship. At the same time, she knows in her God-created spirit that she needs a man strong enough to help her face things about herself which she would otherwise avoid if left to herself. She needs a man capable and willing to wield the sword of truth with a manly sensitivity, that is, with the courage to cut where and when necessary, and with the love to do it with respect for her and submission to the God who has created them both.

Al and Janet, for example, came to me after battling to a standoff since the previous Saturday's family trip to an amusement park.

"It was a real horror show," Al declared, glowering at Janet.

"As soon as we got out of the driveway she began telling me which way to turn, how fast to drive—the works. She just kept harping on me the whole day and never let up!"

I was about to invite Janet's response when she spoke up readily. "It's true," she said matter-of-factly. "Al's right. I was a bitch all day." Hesitating, Janet looked at me with a mixture of sadness and frustration, then dropped her eyes.

I turned to Al. "What did you do when your wife began verbally assaulting you like that?"

"Well . . . I just kind of backed off and figured she'd lay off before long." Al shifted uneasily.

"And did that work?"

Al shook his head and sighed, now angry more at the situation than with his wife.

"Janet," I said, "what were you needing from Al at that moment in the car when you began criticizing him so much? What do you wish he might have done besides just pulling away and clamming up?"

Gently, vulnerably, Janet spoke to her husband. "I wish . . . you'd just tried to stop me somehow." Al sat up in surprise as Janet continued. "I wish . . . you could've said something to me about how bad I was acting. I mean, I was out of control and . . . I needed you to help me get back in control of myself."

Al was amazed. "You mean you *wanted* me to speak up like that? But . . ."

"I know," Janet said. "You're afraid I'll just get angry back at you—and maybe I will at first. But I need you to hang in there with me and not give up."

Sensing that neither partner had a vocabulary for such confrontation in a spirit of love, I spoke to both. "What if Al were to say something like, 'Janet, you're really coming on awfully strong right now, and I'm spending all my energy trying to defend myself rather than dealing with the situation. If there's something specific you're angry about, tell me and let's talk it over. But if not, why not just let go of it and let's enjoy the day together?'"

Janet sighed. "Yeah . . . I need that kind of telling me the truth without putting me down the same way I'm putting Al down."

Al needed to recognize the spirit of fear and condemnation—not Janet—as the true enemy.

Clearly, Al had no model for seeing his masculine strength as an agent of healing. He was sensitive enough to reject the macho image of violence in response to the woman's anger, but he had not yet appropriated the courage and strength of the biblical model that urges "speaking the truth in a spirit of love" (Eph. 4:15). As we discussed this, it became clear why not: Al's mother had been a volatile, angry woman when he was a boy, and he had grown up fearing the woman's anger. His father, predictably, had simply withdrawn from his mother's outbursts, even abandoning Al to her fury. And so Al's manly courage and strength in the face of his wife's anger simply lay dormant under considerable childhood fear.

Al began to move from fear into courageous love as I invited him to ask Jesus to help him in a prayer exercise of telling his mother how much she frightened him as a boy. As he did so, the Holy Spirit showed him how his mother's own brokenness from her girlhood was fueling her anger, and he was able to forgive her. Then, similarly, he told his father in prayer how abandoned he felt as a boy. To his surprise, the Spirit showed him his father as a boy before his grandmother, in virtually the same fearful pattern. Now fully in touch with his own pain, he was able to recognize it in part as his father's pain as well, and to forgive him.

And then, at last, we called upon the Father God to fulfill in Al the manly courage and strength which he longed for.

Another woman who fumed at me about her husband may have summarized the female perspective on such situations:

Whenever I get angry, he just backs off. He's so . . . wimpy! If he's afraid of me and my anger, how's he ever going to help me when I'm in real trouble?

Colleen, a friend of mine who has two master's degrees and oversees a large office, expressed the positive effects of such genuine manliness in her boyfriend Brian. "What I really appreciate about Brian," she said, "is when I get kind of hyper sometimes, anxious and running off at the mouth, and he says to me in a calm, direct voice, 'You know, you're really running at high speed right now.' That gives me the reality check, the balance I need, and lets me calm down and get back on course where I want to be."

Clearly, Brian is not afraid of the woman's energy, and is therefore able to intervene in the face of it with the Word of truth—which sets the woman free to focus her energy more appropriately, and thus feel better about herself.

Hence, the sword heals.

All too often, however, like John at the outset of this chapter, the man balks at exercising such strength with the woman, because he fears, "If I get strong with her, she will leave me." Such hesitation reflects the boy's fear of the mother who, when she sees her son's growing up and away from her, may threaten to withdraw affection from him by pouting or manipulating against his growing strength in an effort to hold onto him. The boy assumes naively that his budding manly strength is a bad thing, because it hurts his mother. He is forced apparently to choose between his manhood and the woman's love—and without a father to stand with him in manly truth, he can only abdicate his strength to the woman.

Thus the true character of a man's later relationship with a particular woman is revealed when he decides at last to exercise his true manly strength with her, as Brian did with Colleen. In all cases, the woman will at first resist his new strength, for it threatens her control over him and the relationship. The woman of God—that is, the one with whom God's purposes for his life can be fulfilled—will eventually recognize his strength as what she's needed, and desire him the more. The woman of the flesh—the one who has merely replaced his mother—will leave him. At that, the man must either surrender to the mother and pursue the woman as a fearful boy, or surrender to the Father

God in order to let go of her and pursue his own, authentic manhood.

The woman thereby longs for her man to desire and seize his own manly sensitivity, because she knows that the only kind she can release in him is her own—which can meet her where she is, true, but cannot take her where she needs to go. If Brian, for example, had only been capable of nurturing Colleen, he might have said to himself, *Poor Colleen is really upset and nervous right now; I don't want to upset her further by interrupting, so I'll just put my arms around her.* Colleen, however, would most likely have pushed him away and become more upset. For what she really needed was a "check" on her spirit, a reflection of what she was doing, a manly word of truth.

In a very real sense, therefore, every woman is a princess held captive by a wicked stepmother—the false feminine maternal-source which would keep her bound as a self-centered child. She longs for a prince who is both strong and bold enough to cut her free from that falseness, so that she can be restored to the "true mother," as it were—the root of authentic femininity.

At the same time, the man must love and respect her even when in her natural fear of new and authentic womanhood, she may at times choose the stepmother over him and refuse to recognize and affirm the healing power in his manly strength—as Colleen was able to do for Brian. Hence, as author Pierre Mornell notes, the "wild woman" often fights back even against the man who would set her free.

Certainly, the woman herself may have been wounded as a girl, perhaps by her father's destructive anger, or by his physical or emotional absence, which denied her a positive model of masculine strength. She therefore may not be able to accept firm, manly sensitivity—such as Brian's—as being helpful, but can only see it as a threat or a sham. In this case, the man must decide how long to persist and when lovingly to let go and separate from the woman for a time, until she genuinely wants to leave the "wicked stepmother." Clearly, a man who fears losing the woman cannot exercise such strength.

Standing before the woman in the strength of manly sensitivity is no small task for a man today. In fact, any men who would ask, "What's in it for the prince?" have already disqualified themselves. For the answer is no more and no less than the satisfaction of authentic manliness, gained by pleasing one's Lord.

This cannot be overemphasized: the man who would lift the sword of truth before the woman must be submitted to his God and seeking to please Him alone. For the woman will often fight and resist him. If he seeks only to please her, he will meekly back off—and thus abandon her to the lie. If he seeks only to please himself, he will resort to coercion and threats—and thus drive her deeper into the lie, resisting him and the truth he bears.

Yet the Church has not offered men the true picture of Jesus in His manly strength.

Often, the all-too-common image of Jesus as a meek and gentle milk-toast character hampers Christian men in orienting themselves toward Him. We rarely stop to consider that no such man could have inspired brawny fishermen like Peter to follow Him. Yet Jesus is ready, indeed, he longs for the opportunity to restore His presence to men as one of manly courage and strength.

I saw this demonstrated dramatically over a period of several weeks in a man who came to me one day brimming with rage at his wife. "She just demands more and more of me the harder I try!" he exclaimed, resentfully detailing how he would come home from an exhausting eight-hour workday to do vacuuming, dishwashing, and other housework chores, even though his wife had been at home all day herself.

I asked Sam if he had ever told his wife directly that he felt unappreciated and taken advantage of.

He had not.

As we talked further, Sam's fear of speaking up for himself became clear, and eventually we agreed to lay that fear before the Lord and ask how He wanted to heal it. Soon after we began praying, Sam recalled an incident at the boarding school which he had attended as a boy. He had refused to take castor oil as ordered by the headmaster, and the latter physically threw him down on the floor of the cafeteria before the other boys and, with a knee in Sam's chest, force-fed him.

I asked Sam if he were willing to invite Jesus into that scene, and he said yes. I waited a moment, and suddenly, Sam buried his face in his hands and cried out, "Oh, no! No!"

"What's happening?" I asked quickly.

"Black-hooded people are in a circle around me and they're coming for me," he exclaimed. "The headmaster is one of them. He comes up close to me and throws back his hood—and it's a horrible snake monster underneath! Oh, no!"

Immediately, I sensed that the enemy had been working through the headmaster when he had so cruelly shamed Sam as a boy before his friends, and I urged Sam to call out the name of Jesus.

Rocking back and forth in fear, he managed to whisper, "Jesus. . . ."

"Again!" I said sharply. "Call out for Jesus!"

"Jesus," he said audibly, and then again, louder, "Jesus!"

I prayed in the Spirit, waiting, as Sam eased back into his chair and became quiet.

After a few moments, Sam spoke up in a tone of wonder and awe. "When I called out for Jesus, a man on a white horse, carrying a big sword, comes along and sends all the guys in black hoods away!" He paused, knitting his brow in confusion. "But I don't understand—this guy is muscular, with big, broad shoulders. He's no wimpy guy at all! In fact, he's got his sword in one hand and drawing me along with the other as he routs the hooded guys. He's not embracing me exactly, or even protecting me, but he's bringing me along, as if I were *part of the battle!!*"

I encouraged Sam to begin letting Jesus be strong and manly, and to let Him draw Sam into His courage and strength over the next week, and I prayed that Sam would let the truth of what Jesus had shown him that day be a balm to Sam's wounded masculine spirit.

The next week, Sam reported that he had been more assertive at work and at home, but that his wife "just flares right back at me even now that I've started telling her up front how I feel."

I had sensed for some time that in order to walk in the Lord's full strength as a husband, Sam would need to pray for her with conviction. "Obviously you're still very angry at your wife," I said, "and we could sit here the whole hour as you tell me why. But sooner or later, you need to recognize that she is not the enemy, but a victim of her own past hurts, just like you."

"Does that mean I just have to go on giving in to her, out of pity?" Sam shot back.

"Not at all. It means that, as you speak up about your own needs and feelings to her, you must be willing to take up the sword in her behalf. That's walking in Jesus' strength."

Sam hesitated. "Well, . . . OK," he said finally. "I do love her and want her to be healed, too."

"Why don't we just ask Jesus how He's praying for her?" I suggested. I then released both Sam and his wife to the Lord, asked Jesus to show Sam how He was praying for her, and prayed in the Spirit, myself.

Moments later, Sam let out a deep sigh, and when I opened my eyes to look at him, I saw he was smiling. I waited until I sensed a release from the Lord, and then asked, "What are you seeing, Sam? Did the Lord show you how He's praying for her?"

"I see a lion," Sam began, smiling broadly. "He's big and strong, with fire coming out of his mouth."

I saw no fear in Sam's face. "Is it a good lion, or a bad one?"

"Good! I'm standing behind him, and I've got a shield in my hand. He's urging me to come out with him. There are dark shapes out there, but he's walking out . . . and I'm following!"

For some time, we talked about this image of the lion and God's strength—and then suddenly it struck me: all this had come in response to a very specific prayer, namely, to let Sam see how the Lord was praying for his wife. I had expected the Lord to give Sam images of his wife, perhaps lonely or afraid. But instead, He had given the lion.

Lord, I asked, *how does the lion demonstrate how You are praying for Sam's wife?* I invited Sam to join me in praying for an answer. Almost at once it came—as if the Lord were saying, "My prayer for her is that her husband walk in My strength. This is

My best hope for her, that he see the true enemy and battle him, not her."

Later that week, Sam's wife called me and asked for an appointment. "It's obvious Sam's getting stronger, speaking up for himself and letting me know how he feels," she said, hesitating. "I know I've always wanted him to be that way . . . but . . . I guess there's a part of me that kind of enjoyed always having the upper hand, and being able to manipulate him into doing what I wanted. I want to be strong enough myself so I don't do that any more."

5
From Love Bug to Faith:
Sexuality and Spirituality

THE ROOT OF MOST problems in man-woman relationships today is our unwillingness to recognize the spiritual dimension of sexuality.

A friend of mine portrayed one of the most pressing such problems in our "modern" age when he called me after an argument with his wife and declared in frustration, "I just don't understand it: we love each other, and yet it's so hard for us to feel like we're really sharing together. It seems like we're always accusing the other, 'You're not giving as much to me as I'm giving to you.'" He paused, exasperated. "There's just *got* to be some way to have a really mutual relationship, where you see the other's need and just give, without being afraid the other's going to take advantage of you!"

My friend was reflecting a common and basic frustration in marriages today. Furthermore, I believe our biblical faith has a vital word of freedom and renewal for such men and women who long for genuine mutuality in their relationships.

Truly hearing that word of faith, however, requires a perspective which is altogether different from that of the world we live in. This was brought into clear focus for me some years ago during the "computer dating" craze, when I read a newspaper article about an enterprising fellow who had patented a pocket-sized device which he called "The Love Bug."

It works like the beepers that doctors carry: you program it with the kind of person you are and the kind of mate you're seeking; whenever you get within range of someone whose Love Bug program matches your specifications—at a party, a singles bar, or a supermarket—the two beepers go off and . . . *voila!* Instant, scientifically certified compatibility.

For some, the Love Bug heralds a brave, new world rid at last of messy feelings and decisions. But if somewhere inside you the Love Bug beeper sounds a warning that makes you pause and wonder, then you're on the path toward understanding the biblical view of sexual difference and attraction.

All of us know that feeling of being attracted to the opposite sex. But where does such a powerful, involuntary force of attraction come from? Popular answers like "magnetism" or "falling in love" suggest that this power which is activated when boy meets girl is greater than any individual, and originates somewhere beyond our conscious human will.

Indeed, for thousands of years, human beings have understood that sexual attraction is so fraught with mystery, so charged with unexplainable power—the power of creation itself—that it cannot be approached without a spiritual perspective. When you deal with strange powers that originate beyond human will, you are in the province of the gods. In fact, the Canaanite tribes in the land Israel eventually occupied felt that sex was so sacred that they "ordained" temple prostitutes with whom a man or woman worshiper might call forth such religious experience.

Only when the God of Israel had spoken was humankind reminded what this power of attraction is, where it comes from, and why it focuses within a covenant which names the Creator

God of the Universe as the binding agent. Even today, our secular culture affirms this basic spiritual dimension of sexuality when we use the religious terms "fidelity" or "faithful" to describe a relationship in which a man and woman limit their sexual expression to the other person, alone.

In the very beginning of the Bible, we read the key conclusion: "For this reason a man will leave his father and his mother and be united with his wife, and they become one flesh" (Gen. 2:24 NIV). Why, indeed? What impels man and woman toward one another in the first place?

Eve was taken from Adam's own body; earlier in Genesis, we read that God "created human beings, making them to be like himself. He created them male and female" (1:27). God, then, is somehow a combination, a union of both male and female. In both the primal, cosmic sense and the individual experience of conception, life originated and originates in a unity of male and female.

And so, in Adam and Eve, the story says that human creation began when God split His own image into two separate parts, male and female—and *that is why* a man and woman are moved toward one another: to reunite and become one flesh, in the original image of God's wholeness.

Today, therefore, as always, we are drawn to the opposite sex not to make babies, not to perpetuate the species, but because from the roots of our creation we share a sacred memory of the species, an ancient inner-recall that at one time we were man-and-woman, Adam-and-Eve, in one body. And so even now the very power of the Creating God is drawing us back to that primal state so we can know God completely, as God was in the beginning, is now, and ever shall be. *That* is where the mysterious, involuntary urge comes from; *that* is why a man and woman are moved to unite sexually.

Sexual desire is an archetypal recall, the voice of the Creator Spirit-God crying out, "Come back, return from your separateness to the oneness out of which I created you."

Clearly, leaving father and mother—as the biblical faith affirms—is essential to this process. For within the emotional force field of Mommy and Daddy, the essential spiritual dimension of the memory is lost, subsumed by the overwhelming desire in the child of the flesh to go back to Mommy and Daddy instead of to venture out into the terrifying desert wilderness of relationship with the other. Yet, as the story of the Exodus notes, only amid fearful uncertainty do we reach out for and discover at last God's saving hand. The essential marriage covenant between God and His people was made in the desert: "you were my bride in the wilderness," as Jeremiah puts it (2:2 NEB).

Sexuality, therefore, is fearful business, because it implies an encounter with the Living God—and, as the cross indicates, encountering the fullness of God's power means being stripped of the security of our own human power.

This fear of one another as men and women is the greatest block to the mutuality we long for together. For myself, that fear first leapt out at me in my high school freshman P.E. class on rainy days, when outdoor sports gave way to folk dancing in the gym with the girls. In those awkward days of budding sexuality, I was the youngest in my class and always the shortest.

Even today, every time I hear "Turkey in the Straw" I freeze inside, recalling the awful tension as we fifty-odd boys lined up by height against one wall of the gym while the girls did likewise opposite us. To my utter fear and embarrassment, the last girl in line opposite me, short though she was, had nevertheless blossomed into precocious abundance. Of course, all the other boys made a great show of wishing they were the shortest, like me, but I now believe they were all secretly glad they did not have to match up against such a young woman themselves. I have also come to realize now that the girls were just as afraid of us as we boys were of them.

Because I believe most of us know that fear from the onset of sexual desire in puberty, I would ask a simple question: what were we—the youngest of men and women—afraid of there in that gym? We all know the answer, because we do not lose that fear with age; we simply become more adept at covering it up.

For myself, the answer is simple: I didn't want to be rejected. I felt very inadequate at relating to girls, and the closer I got to them, the more inadequate I felt. Sure, we boys could all tell great stories among the other guys . . . but when it's just the two of you there alone, boy and girl, all the fears of not measuring up, of weakness and uncertainty, tremble within.

The motivational power which this fear wields in our lives has not been lost upon the powers of the world, for commercial advertising depends largely on that fear for its effectiveness. Ads aimed at women, describing such things as nylons, perfumes, and jewelry, often show the woman purchaser moving boldly around the man, even mesmerizing him—and in control of the otherwise fearful powers that the man evokes.

Car ads for men often picture an attractive woman nearby. The woman brings out sexual desire in the male customer. Yet those desires are bound up in fears of inadequacy and rejection; the female model is chosen because she is more attractive than any woman normally available to the male customer. In the presence of the fearful powerlessness which the attractive woman elicits, the car is touted for its "maneuverability" and "ease of handling." The message is clear: power to control the car compensates for the fear of having no power to control the woman, of being vulnerable before her. Hence men are drawn to powerful machines.

In the movie *The Right Stuff*, for example, test pilot Chuck Yeager risks his life almost casually in manmade flying machines, and confesses to his wife the only thing he's ever been afraid of in life: "You."

How, indeed, are we men and women to deal with this awesome fear between us which undermines mutuality and togetherness?

The powers of the world offer a ready answer: make sex a purely physical, material thing, as with the Love Bug; then you can control and manage it just as physical human power controls other things. Advertising accomplishes this by continually prompting sexual desire with suggestive pictures and associating that desire with material products. It's like Pavlov's dogs, who were fed as he rang a bell, until eventually they salivated simply at the sound of a bell, without any food present. That is, if you present a sexy person along with your product long enough, soon the customer will experience sexual attraction upon seeing your product, without any person of the opposite sex present.

Biblical faith, however, offers a quite different answer to our fear of sexuality: recognize its fundamentally spiritual nature, and submit it to the God who "is Spirit" (John 4:24), for His guidance. As Paul told the early Christians at Ephesus: "Submit yourselves to one another because of your reverence for Christ" (5:22).

Insofar as Christ is God's Word of truth which "cuts all the way through, to where soul and spirit meet" (Heb. 4:12), a young engaged man whose wedding I performed provided me with a major clue to understanding this. "I think I've figured out why we get defensive sometimes and either pull away or fight," he said about his relationship with his fiancée. "We're really not being honest with each other. I mean, the truth I'm really afraid to say to her is this: 'I love you, and that means I just can't close off to you, no matter how hard I try. The more I love you, the more attached and open I am, and the more I get afraid that you won't love me as much as I love you—and I'll be left standing there open, vulnerable, and alone.'"

Here, I believe, is the major stumbling block to genuine mutuality in marriage: "How can I relax and be open with you, if I'm afraid you haven't got as much invested in this relationship as I do? If I'm the one taking all the risk and you're ready to pull away at any time?" A few years ago I saw a survey which indicated that in marriages today, power is seen as belonging to the partner who has the most credible threat of withdrawing from the relationship. The least committed one, that is, has the most power.

In the model of Christ, however, the most committed One becomes the channel for the power of God in the relationship. Jesus was vulnerable unto death, and therefore became the authentic channel for the power of life over death in a self-centered world.

We may thank God that Jesus did not turn away from the Cross saying, "I'm afraid I have more invested in this relationship than you." Instead, the biblical faith understands that this is precisely why God sent His Son: because we human beings aren't willing to take much risk at all in our relationship with God, but insist on clinging to our own plans and schemes which nevertheless lead us to death. Wonder of wonders: it was while we were "yet sinners" that Christ died for us. Yet we continue to insist that we can live in a loving relationship only if the other person risks as much as we.

The Good News of our Christian faith, therefore, is that our fear of one another, our fear of being vulnerable and rejected or abandoned, was met by Jesus Christ on the cross. If anybody had the right to pull out of a relationship, it was the betrayed Jesus; if anybody had the right to call down legions of angels in revenge, it was the rejected, abandoned Jesus. Yet Jesus walked the path to the Cross, which terrifies our self-centered human nature. He opened the door by which we may risk such vulnerability in our loving relationships today—trusting not that the other partner will change, but that God will not change His saving power for those who love as He loves in Christ.

As long as we submit ourselves to Christ, we have the power to love this boldly. Our fear of the other's rejection, therefore, is overcome by our faith in God—not, as the world insists, by reducing our sexuality to a manageable, material thing.

The world defines an acceptable relationship as one in which each partner risks the same investment, and is therefore no more vulnerable than the other. Love becomes a fifty-fifty contract in which he paid for dinner last time, she pays this time; he listened to her problem last time, she listens to his this time.

Our human standard of mutuality requires that each partner gets what he or she wants out of the relationship. But the Christian standard, according to the model of Jesus, is that each partner gives what God wants, namely, reverence for Christ. And out of our willingness to revere Christ and follow in His way, we are set free to submit to one another without fear.

In our human flesh, we are afraid to submit to the one we love for fear of losing ourselves in the other person and thus have no identity of our own. And indeed, without being submitted to Christ, this is not simply a danger, but the true and natural consequence. You abdicate your own self and give your partner the power to define you—something which only God can do.

But the promise of our faith to loving relationships is this: the man who is first submitted to Christ is then free to submit to the woman according to His leading; that is, his sacrifice gives God power over the relationship, even as over his individual life.

From a Christian perspective, then, marriage requires not equitable independence, but rather, mutual submission—which begins with each partner's being submitted to Christ. When we begin with reverence for Christ, we can submit to the other without fear. When left to our own devices, however, we have reverence only for our own well-being, and in our hearts we "keep score." Our self-centered human nature requires that the other person always come out with a lower score than we do. Hence, we feel taken advantage of and unwilling to give any more.

When you have given yourself to Jesus Christ, you know that you belong to God, and you need no longer fear losing yourself in your partner. You can begin to let God shape for His purposes not only yourself as an individual, but your marriage as well.

What does it mean for a man in love with a woman to have "reverence for Christ"?

It means that he must go to the Cross. It means he must kneel before the vulnerable, rejected, abandoned Lord of heaven and earth, and pour out his brokenness and fear to Him, awaiting His direction. It means crying out, "Lord, I give up. I'm tired of wasting energy with the woman I love defending my pride, afraid of losing power to her, struggling to act 'manly.' I give myself to You first, Lord—not to her; make me the man You want me to be."

I believe that God is calling men and women to a new spirit of mutuality in the eighties and nineties. It is not the call of the fifties for women to submit to men, nor the call of the sixties for men to submit to women. And it is not the call of the seventies to submit to no one and look out instead for "number one." It is instead the ancient, enduring call of the Loving Creator for us men and women to submit ourselves to one another out of

reverence for Christ—that is, to turn to the Living God, so that
we might turn to one another without fear and become the
agents of love we were created to be.

Those men who dare walk in such humility, trust, and truth
before God will discover at last the authentic "fear" which the
woman's presence engenders: not that she might reject him, but
that his physical attraction heralds the awesome, "fearful" presence of the Living God and His call to surrender—not to the
woman, nor to the desires of our flesh, but to Him. In fact, we *are*
inadequate in relating sexually to the woman, because doing so
places us in the realm of the spirit, where we have no power of
our own.

Until we have learned to accept this essential spiritual nature
of our sexual attraction, we remain easy prey to the urgings of our
self-centered flesh. Those men who have learned this lesson are
ready now to face the ever-present question, "How do I deal with
my sexual attraction to a woman when it seems both overwhelming and inappropriate?"

6
To
Corral
the
Stallion

The Lord asked, "Why should I forgive the sins of my people? They have abandoned me and have worshiped gods that are not real. I fed my people until they were full, but they committed adultery and spent their time with prostitutes. They were like well-fed stallions wild with desire, each lusting for his neighbor's wife. Shouldn't I punish them for these things and take revenge on a nation such as this? (Jer. 5:7–9).

IN RECENT YEARS, the nation's headlines have blared out a number of major stories about men who had violated their high positions of trust through sexual impropriety.

In religion, PTL television ministry founder Jim Bakker confessed to having solicited a prostitute and authorized a quarter-million dollars for hush money out of his ministry. Televangelist Jimmy Swaggart was caught with a prostitute. Both Swaggart and

Bakker were disgraced and once again the carnality of church leaders offered a nation of disbelievers more ammunition to wield against the faith.

In national defense, Marine guards at the American embassy in Moscow were discovered to have allowed Soviet agents into top-secret areas after being seduced by women spies. Millions of dollars spent on a new embassy building were considered wasted, as security plans for it were leaked to the Russians, and our national strength against enemies was held up to ridicule.

In politics, front-running Democratic presidential candidate Gary Hart mocked all standards of public morality as he took an actress young enough to be his daughter on overnight yacht cruises. Hart was forced to drop out of the presidential race, and the Democratic party was thrown into confusion at a time when it might easily have capitalized on the declining popularity of the Republican president.

Lest anyone believe the popular notion that a man's sexual behavior is exclusively his "own private business," with no larger effects on society, these examples testify convincingly to the contrary. Indeed, they demonstrate clearly Jeremiah's prophetic biblical witness that private morality has profound public consequences—even altering the course of careers, ministries, and nations.

Nor can these "national" incidents be seen as isolated. They reflect a festering sexual insecurity among men throughout our society. Today, more and more men are willing to risk destroying family, career, ministry, nation—and themselves—all for a few moments of physical gratification with a woman. Perhaps such a man fancies himself as a bold macho figure, demonstrating sexual prowess. But he is actually a male child abdicating his manly initiative and strength to the woman.

Among earlier generations, popular male mythology held that in all cases the woman was cleverly deceived by the man, with his superior power. Certainly, the female nymphomaniac flourished in locker room lore; but in real life, male efforts worthy of esteem focused on "how to get her to go along." One enterprising fellow in my high school senior class, for example, used to hold us spellbound with tales of his vodka ice cubes, secreted in dry ice until the critical moment, when he would administer them to his girlfriend's Coca-cola®. Of course, he allowed, the cubes would dissolve instantly, due to alcohol's lower freezing point, but a skilled Lothario such as he could easily divert the woman's attention.

In today's era of so-called "sexual liberation," such tricks would be condemned as patronizing to the woman—who may not only share complicity, but in fact initiate the encounter. In such cases, popular male mythology obliges the man to charge ahead, that is, to move ahead even faster to gain the initiative over the advancing woman.

Yet in doing so, the man abdicates initiative to the woman, to let her desires set the pace. Current sexual mores tend to obscure the essential fact that a man is no more obliged to respond to a woman's advances than a woman is to a man's. Discipline and self-control are as essential to the warrior in the "battle of the sexes" as they are in any conflict. Often the enemy would draw us out prematurely in order to expose our flank (literally, in this context) for the kill. The reader who might object here to the military metaphor needs only to consider the embassy Marines, whose unwillingness to say no to the female Russian spies may have endangered far more lives than any individual act of cowardice on the battlefield.

Indeed, Jesus came to earth to battle for human souls. Sexual relationships, based on the profoundly spiritual dimension of sexuality itself, therefore become a primary context for that conflict. Contrary to the world's view, however, the "battle of the sexes" is not between the man and the woman, one trying to dominate the other; it is between God and the self-centered desires of the "flesh" in *both* man and woman. Victory in that battle was won by Jesus on the cross, when He yielded His body to the God who created it. The Good News in this for men and women is that those couples who have surrendered themselves to Jesus at the cross are freed from the urgent demands of their self-centered human nature to love like Jesus—for the other's sake and not their own.

In our male hearts we know it is not the woman who must be dominated, but the masculine power, which, when unbridled, leads to destruction not only of self but of others, as in war and adultery. We fear not the woman's power, but our own. We run from the lion, because we know we cannot in our own human strength dominate or control our masculine power. Only as we turn it over to Jesus—when it becomes His, even as it becomes Him, the Lion of Judah—are we freed from fearing it, so we can focus it for His creative, restoring purposes.

A man therefore becomes most concerned about dominating or controlling the woman when he has refused to let Jesus dominate him. When, on the other hand, a man yields his masculine power of the flesh to Jesus, it becomes a tool in Jesus' hands. The man's energy is no longer consumed in maneuvering against the woman's apparent power to control him, but in serving Jesus—in walking with the Lion instead of running from Him.

And this Lion is neither a spineless milk-toast nor a Rambo run amok. He is as likely to embrace the woman even though she lashes out and hurts him, as to say no and call her to accountability—depending on the Father God's desire and initiative.

Hell may indeed have no fury like a woman scorned. But Heaven reserves due blessing for the man who submits his sexuality to the Father God instead of to the woman and the desires of the flesh.

The so-called "Playboy philosophy," for example, focuses on the enticing Playmate. The good news of the Playboy gospel is that the woman confers masculinity upon the reader by sexually arousing him with her "come-on" posture. In reality, however, the reader has simply yielded his manly initiative to the woman and her desires. He has given his masculine spirit over to the goddess and thus, lost it.

The Good News of Jesus Christ, on the other hand, proclaims that the Father God confers masculinity upon the man who humbles himself in response to Jesus' posture on the Cross. By yielding his natural desires to the Father God, the believer gives his masculine spirit over to the Father God and thus, gains it—it becomes subject to him, rather than he to it.

We men today must be weaned away from the popular notion, ranging in expression from pornographic magazines to cheerleaders, that a woman can confer manhood upon us. The woman's admiration and desire is a *consequence* of our authentic manhood—not the source of it. Like the black widow spider who lures the male to copulate only to kill him afterward, the woman who discovers she can manipulate a man through her sexual charms will disrespect him and destroy his manhood eventually—just as the female Russian spy disgraced the embassy Marines. Granted, the man who does not respond to the woman's advances may face a fury like unto hell itself. But the man who has not learned to face the fury of hell in the power of the crucified and risen Lord—who balks at raising the sword of God's truth—is no mature son of the Father God, and therefore has no business relating to women sexually in the first place.

Without the earthly father to call the boy out into manhood, the boy grows up seeking manly identity in women—whose voices seem to call him to manhood through sexual conquest. But this is a deception that has been recognized by men for thousands of years, as in the ancient myth of the Siren women, who cried out for sailors only to dash their ship upon the rocks. Masculinity grows not out of conquering the woman, but only out of conquering the man—and not another man, as in war, but oneself.

Christian men understand that they cannot in their own human power, overcome themselves and the natural desires of their flesh. As Paul lamented, "I know that good does not live in me—that is, in my human nature. For even though the desire to do good is in me, I am not able to do it" (Rom. 7:18). The focus of human willpower must be toward turning ourselves over to Jesus, who alone can conquer us in God's way—by nailing our proud human nature to the cross. Paul said: "What an unhappy man I am! Who will rescue me from this body that is taking me to death? Thanks be to God, who does this through our Lord Jesus Christ!" (Rom. 7:24, 25).

Certainly, every man knows the seemingly overwhelming power of sexual desire, which can indeed deliver him over to the powers of death and destruction—as with Gary Hart, Jim Bakker,

Jimmy Swaggart, and the Marine guards at the U.S. embassy in Moscow. Unfortunately, every man does not know the overruling power of Jesus Christ, who can deliver him into the Father God's powers of life and authentic manhood.

Perhaps the greatest block to understanding that saving power of Jesus Christ is the Law. Most men know the Commandment, "You shall not commit adultery." In this broken world not yet submitted to God's rule, adulterous impulses and occasions will present themselves to all of us at times. The man who lives under the Law will at such times grit his teeth, bite the bullet, and battle the impulse, perhaps even condemning himself for having such thoughts. He walks in constant fear of failing. With no other dispensation available, certainly the Law is better than nothing. But sooner or later the man who acknowledges only the Law may either burn himself out grinding his teeth, or give up and yield to sin. In any case, his lot is not an enviable one.

Under the New Covenant initiated by Jesus, another avenue has opened for lasting saving power. Through Jesus' death and resurrection, the powers separating us from God—namely, our self-centered pride that leads us to sin—have been overcome. We no longer live by threat of the Law, but by the promise of the Holy Spirit, who empowers us to draw close to God and overcome our desires of the flesh.

Argentine pastor-author Juan Carlos Ortiz has expressed this powerfully in noting that "the Law gives commandments; grace gives promises."[1] He holds up the promise of the Father God for the New Covenant even through the prophets of the Old Covenant:

> I will sprinkle clean water upon you, and you shall be clean from all your uncleanness. . . . I will put my spirit within you, and cause you to walk in my statutes and be careful to observe my ordinances (Ezek. 36:25, 27 RSV).

As Ortiz declares,

> God promises that we are going to be able, that we are going to be careful to observe His ordinances. The Law says, "You shall not

commit adultery." Grace says, "I promise that you will not commit adultery."

For witness to this promise in the New Covenant, he notes Peter's reassurance:

> God's divine power has given us everything we need to live a truly religious life through our knowledge of the one who called us to share in his own glory and goodness. In this way he has given us the very great and precious gifts he promised, so that by means of these gifts you may escape from the destructive lust that is in the world, and may come to share the divine nature (2 Peter 1:3, 4).

Ortiz then portrays a dialogue response from the Christian man who hears this promise that he shall indeed not commit adultery:

> Man: Who, me? How come?
> God: Because now I am in you.
> M: Yes, but . . .
> G: Why don't you trust me? Come on, believe this. Say, "I will not commit adultery."
> M: Lord, I cannot assure that . . .
> G: Then you have no faith. "The just shall live by faith." I've given you my precious and magnificent promises that you may become like me, without sin. Come on, believe me!

Underscoring the necessity for the individual man to commit his own will in God's direction through such faith, Ortiz offers an analogy to power brakes: we need only decide to put our foot on the pedal and push; once we do that much, God's power takes over and does the "braking" on our impulses as necessary. "When the man sees that nice, attractive lady," Ortiz says, "he can say, 'In the name of Jesus, No!' He will be delighted, overjoyed to discover that is all that is necessary."

Clearly, neither Gary Hart, Jim Bakker, Jimmy Swaggart, or the embassy Marines exercised this promise of God—any more than most men today do. For we have not acknowledged that sexual union is something God ordains, not something which human desire dictates. The man who, on the other hand, yields himself to the Father God may trust not only that God will "cause him to be careful" not to fall, but that God will bring him to sexual union with the proper woman if he walks in trust and obedience. Such a walk in faith takes the edge off the urgency of a man's sexual desire, and thereby makes him less vulnerable to temptation.

While the individual man's commitment to such faith is essential, we must draw upon the collective courage and strength of fellow brothers in our faith walk. A man out of fellowship with other godly men fools only himself in thinking he can grow as God's son all by himself.

The Bible portrays this warning clearly in the story of King David and Bathsheba. When David succumbed to the temptation, he was basically alone in the city, not out with his men where he should have been:

> The following spring, at the time of the year when kings usually go to war, David sent out Joab with his officers and the Israelite army; they defeated the Ammonites and besieged the city of Rabbah. But David himself stayed in Jerusalem (2 Sam. 11:1).

Why wasn't David out in the field with his men, as was expected of the king? We are not told; we only know that while his men were suffering on the battlefield, David was luxuriating in afternoon naps and strolls around the palace roof—from which he spotted Bathsheba as might a common peeping Tom. Having thus eschewed the company of fellow men, he lost his warrior's sense of discipline and concern for their welfare.

In the depravity of his unmanliness, when he learned she was pregnant, David called home Bathsheba's husband Uriah from the battlefront, hoping Uriah would sleep with her and David's own perfidy would be cloaked. But Uriah offered the positive model of the warrior, which David had turned from, and refused to sleep with his wife, explaining,

> The men of Israel and Judah are away in battle, and the Covenant Box is with them; my commander Joab and his officers are camping

out in the open. How could I go home, eat and drink, and sleep with my wife? By all that's sacred, I swear that I could never do such a thing! (2 Sam. 11:11).

Uriah is a picture of the man of God, submitted to the Father, in fellowship with the men of God. He understood and submitted to the discipline of that fellowship, acknowledging its precedence over his sex drive—even when it would apparently break no commandment to exercise it.

Surely, many American allies in wartime have wished that we had reared more Uriahs in our Army, considering the numbers of pregnant women and single mothers our soldiers often leave behind.

How many young men today, immersed in the "looking-out-for-number-one" hedonism of our modern society, would even consider the manly warrior discipline demonstrated by Uriah? More likely, they would jump at the chance for whatever sexual opportunity that came along. For, unlike Uriah, the modern male has no commitment to a community of fellow warriors who support and encourage his own manly integrity. "After all," they might say, "the king himself said it was OK for Uriah to do it." It would never occur to them that the king, indeed all earthly authority, is ultimately accountable to the Father God, and therefore worthless as a defense in the heavenly court which all men must face.

In the biblical faith, sexual fidelity is first and foremost faithfulness to God, not to the woman. If a man is faithful primarily to the woman, when the natural hurts and angers arise between him and the woman, he will find ample justification for not remaining faithful to her. If, on the other hand, his primary fidelity is to God, he cannot be tempted to sin by his wife's actions, no matter how hurtful they be.

The most pointed example of such faithfulness is reflected in the actions of Joseph, who in fact had no wife at the time, and thus, by the world's standards did not need to be concerned with his own sexual fidelity:

Joseph was well-built and good-looking, and after a while his master's wife began to desire Joseph and asked him to go to bed with

her. He refused and said to her, "Look, my master does not have to
concern himself with anything in the house, because I am here. He
has put me in charge of everything he has. I have as much authority in this house as he has, and he has not kept back anything from
me except you. How then could I do such an immoral thing,
and sin against God?" Although she asked Joseph day after day, he
would not go to bed with her (Gen. 39:6b–10).

The case of Ralph, a young Christian man who sought my
help for his fear of falling to sexual temptation, portrays a remarkably apt resolution to Jeremiah's prophecy against males
consumed by a "stallion's" lust. Married with several children,
Ralph told of a woman at his office who came to him regularly to
tell him "how terribly" her husband "abused" her. When eventually he felt overwhelmed by her problems and sought to back off
from conversations with her, she declared "how terribly" it hurt
her that he would "pull away like that." Feeling guilty, he continued listening to her tales of woe—unaware of her seductive un-
dertones—until he finally realized he was enjoying her attention
and attracted to her.

As we talked, Ralph mentioned that his father had been
considerably older than his mother, and had died when Ralph
was a teenager. Emotionally as well as chronologically distant
from his wife, the father had abdicated his manly responsibility to
meet her need for affection and support. Predictably, she turned
to her son to fill the gap, imposing a host of subtle demands upon
Ralph after his father died.

For several weeks, we prayed to break Ralph's dependency
on his mother and to receive the Father God's manly strength
before women. Though he gained a clear intellectual perspective
on his problem, Ralph seemed unable to receive godly strength
to overcome his weakness around women. To my increasing frustration, in our prayers we received very few visions, words of
prophecy, or special wisdom toward that goal.

One day, soon after Ralph had arrived at my office, we were
settling in with casual conversation and he mentioned a "scary
thing" that had happened to him the previous week. Ralph lived

on a large piece of property on the far edge of the city, and, having been raised on a farm, had some years earlier decided to build a small barn and board horses for extra income and as a change of pace from city life.

One evening he had gone out to check on the horses, and to his dismay, a large stallion had broken out of his stall and was leaping about, trying to break into a nearby mare's stall. Nostrils flared, mane whipping about, and penis fully erect, the stallion thrashed furiously at the wooden gate.

"I was absolutely terrified when I came close enough to see what was going on," Ralph declared. "When he saw me, the stallion reared back and kicked out angrily; I jumped back and my first thought was just to get back to the house and let him do what he would. Still, I had to think of the owner, and my reputation as a horse boarder; the stallion could injure himself kicking away at the gate, and if he got in, he could certainly do things to the mare, whose owner I'd have to answer to."

Ralph shook his head and sighed. "Suddenly, almost without thinking, I spotted a three-foot-long two-by-four nearby. I picked it up, and held it high, shaking it threateningly at the stallion. To my surprise, he snorted and then sort of backed off. He was still hot for that mare, and I was still pretty scared of him. But when he backed up, I gathered my courage and stepped toward him, shaking that two-by-four.

"The door to his stall was open, and I stepped around to kind of guide him back into it. I'm not sure even now how it happened, but before long, he had backed into his stall, and I locked him in."

Ralph was visibly nervous as he spoke, yet a clear tone of strength had entered his voice as he told of shaking the two-by-four at the stallion, and thereby overcoming his fear. In my response as a pastor, I affirmed his experience and thanked him for sharing it. I was just about to shift gears and ask what the day's agenda might be, when it struck me: what more graphic, fearful image of unbridled male sexuality was there than that of a stallion kicking down the gate to the mare's stall? And what more potent image of restraint that Ralph's raising the two-by-four?

"Well anyhow, let's get on with today's session," Ralph was saying.

"Actually," I said, "I think your encounter with the stallion is the real focus of today's session—and all the sessions we've had up till now, in fact!"

Ralph knit his brow, puzzled. "What do you mean?"

Shaking my head in amazement and delight, I explained: "Up till now, we've been focusing on your fear that your sexual feelings might get out of control, right?"

Ralph nodded, still confused.

"Your run-in with the stallion was a perfect occasion for you to face head-on the sense of your own out-of-control male sexuality—the hot and determined stallion in you, so to speak. We've been talking about how you can gain the strength to confront and corral that stallion."

Ralph's face had brightened. "And by God, I did it!" he exclaimed.

"Yes," I said, nodding and smiling with him, "by the grace and power of God, you did it."

Ralph soon confronted the woman at his office gently but firmly, telling her that he agreed she needed help, but that he was not able to give it to her. In fact, he gave her the name of a female therapist I had supplied. She became furious; he wavered, but stood his ground. A few weeks later, when he finally refused to listen to her any more she stomped off, shouting that she would never speak to him again. Ralph fought off feelings of guilt and again stood his ground. Eventually, the woman sought the professional help she needed, and one day months later came to Ralph. "Thank you for what you did, in not putting up with my childishness any longer," she said to him. She is now in therapy and progressing; Ralph, meanwhile, is thrilled with the new sense of power within him.

"I prayed for Jesus to give me the manly strength I never got growing up," he declared, "and now at last He's giving it to me." He paused. "Check that. Now, at last, I'm willing to receive it! For so long, I thought it would only hurt the woman's feelings, like it did with my mother, who couldn't stand to face the truth about her own emptiness and need for my father. Now I realize that my manly strength actually helps the woman as much as it helps me!"

May we men dare to rediscover the power God has given us to raise the sword of truth against the unbridled stallion within us. That is, may we submit our male sexuality to Jesus, who offers us the "yoke" (Matt. 11:29) needed to harness it for the good of ourselves and our nation—that we might then celebrate this biblical benediction:

> To him who is able to keep you from falling and to bring you faultless and joyful before his glorious presence—to the only God our Savior, through Jesus Christ our Lord, be glory, majesty, might, and authority, from all ages past, and now and forever! Amen (Jude 24).

7

Lost Among Men:

A Nonpolitical View of Homosexuality

CARL HAD PAINTED A graphic portrait of his harsh, unemotional father, his clinging mother, and then his own rebellious ways that had ultimately led his father to declare: "You're no son of mine anymore!"

And now, the Lord had raised His sword of truth.

"At the time, I just turned up my nose at Dad and told myself I didn't need his love and approval anyhow," Carl said, shifting uneasily in the chair opposite me. "But . . . now I realize I was doing all those crazy rebellious things mostly because I really longed for it, and was trying to punish him for not giving it to me."

As with all resentful rebellion, however, the one who suffered most was Carl himself—in a way that confused and frightened him.

"A little while after that, I was hitchhiking, and some guy

102

stopped. I went over to get in, and he says pointblank, 'You wouldn't be gay, would you?' I was surprised, but I just backed out of the car and said 'No thanks.' And then, a couple of weeks later, I was at a party and met this middle-aged guy. He invited me to come over to his place, and naively, I went. Before long, he was propositioning me. I could hardly believe it. I tried to be civil, but I got out of there quick."

After a number of similar encounters, Carl began to wonder about himself: *Do I look gay?* In time, the wondering became an abiding fear: *Am I gay?* Though he resolved to resist such a conclusion at all costs, he began having homosexual fantasies, even dreams. "What in the world is happening to me?" he blurted out finally, and then lowered his eyes. "You know, this is what really made me come to you for help weeks ago—not all the other stuff we've been talking about."

Gently, I assured him that the "other stuff" was in fact very important to his fears of being homosexual.

I explained that pushing his father to reject him so "finally" had been a desperate effort to free himself from the constant threat of rejection which the father had held over him for so long. Rather than remain vulnerable to the father's mercurial mercy, not knowing when another word of temporary rejection might strike, Carl had rebelliously sought to control the situation himself, and forced his father to reject him once and for all—to get it over with.

Yet Carl had not counted the cost of his action. Being "finally cut off" from his father did not set him free from fear, as he had hoped. On the contrary, it stripped him of all pretense of denial—with which he had shielded himself from the pain of his father's rejection. And so he was rendered more vulnerable than ever to his inner fears of rejection and his longing for male acceptance and affection. Too proud to focus those fears and longings on his father, where they truly belonged, Carl diligently suppressed them. In doing so, he simply insured that they would surface in false, inappropriate ways, namely, in sexual attraction to other men.

In fact, Carl did have a very real physical need for another man—not just any other man, though, as the homosexual imagines—but one particular man: his father. Furthermore, Carl's need was sexual but not for coitus. What he needed was confirmation of his male sexual identity.

Like any other compulsive activity which might be used to cover up the truth about oneself, homosexuality is not so much a sin as a lie that cannot abide the manly sword of truth.

The incarnation, the "en-flesh-ment" of God in Jesus Christ, reflects the basic truth that spiritual relationship seeks a physical component in this world. A boy's spiritual relationship with his mother is graphically "en-fleshed" in her womb.

Yet the boy also longs for a physical bonding to complement his spiritual bond with the father. As Robert Bly puts it, "a son has a kind of body-longing for the father, which must be honored."[1]

In fact, the boy's "body-longing" for his father may be even more intense than that for the mother, since the boy has at least had nine months of intimate physical contact with her from conception. In any case, the boy needs his daddy to hold him, to hug him, even to tumble and wrestle with him on the living-room floor.

If, however, the father is physically cold and distant, or absent altogether, the boy's longing goes unfulfilled, and prompts anxiety about bonding with other males. In some cases, the boy suppresses into his subconscious the unbearable pain of not having the father's physical affection—only to have it resurface later in a distorted form: sexual desire for other men.

In some cases, the father has abused the son. In any case, the boy who fears his father must fear manhood, and withdraw from it; the boy who hates his father cannot embrace and celebrate his own manliness.

A striking example of how homosexuality is engendered by a controlling mother, quite apart from culture, is offered in playwright Paul Stephen Lim's *Mother Tongue*. As a *Los Angeles Times* reviewer declared,

> There are three mother tongues in this play—Chinese, English, and the angry tongue of the professor's accusatory mother. She figures

prominently in the form of memories and flashbacks that haunt the life of an overseas Chinese . . . who is homosexual. . . .[2]

Referring later to "the punitive mother figure who won't go away," the reviewer notes,

> There are homosexual motifs that bring dimension . . . particularly a nervous, edgy scene with a bold American student . . . accompanied by a fantasy guilt trip from shouting mother—"Why is that boy always following you around?" Also helpful are deft, artfully structured depictions of an old and now shattered male relationship. . . .

Neither the liberal nor conservative view regarding homosexuality serves the healing purposes of God. According to the conservative, it is a sin that must be punished; to the liberal, it is either a free choice, entirely healthy, or a genetic component, no more "wrong" than being black. In praying with many men struggling against homosexual impulses my experience suggests rather that homosexual men suffer the emotional effects of a distant father and a possessive mother. Most often, the boy's father has not helped him break his identification with the mother/woman by calling him out to male fellowship and identity.

From this perspective, both the liberal universalists and the conservative legalists are bedfellows. Regardless of "political" persuasion, every man is a son in search of his father's affection and approval, longing for Daddy's embrace even as his mother "embraced" him in the womb. Yet this vulnerable, wounded little boy within every man threatens his adult pride. In any case, men seek to avoid him. And when he desperately cries out from one who has acted out homosexually, men become determined to eliminate him altogether: the liberals would abandon him under guise of "openness," while the conservatives would quarantine him.

"Political" battles over homosexuality are therefore a sham, mere window dressing to screen the deeper insecurity of a man's inner wounds. Meanwhile, ignored and rejected yet again—his voice muffled by "adult" rationalizations and accusations—the little boy in every man cries out for his father's embrace.

The conservative temptation simply to condemn and reject the homosexual man not only hinders his healing, it exacerbates the cause of his problem. And the liberal effort to excuse his actions as "healthy" only hinders the homosexual's healing process, which requires that he accept responsibility for his actions.

Yet when we see homosexuals glossing over their brokenness as if it were just fine, we are simply observing in another man the same charade, the same rationalizing away of sin—albeit different sin—that we ourselves indulge. Until we recognize and confess this common basis for fellowship under God, we have no right as Christians to speak about the sin of homosexuality. Only a fellow sinner can call another to accountability; in our proud human nature, our only insurance against condemning another is our awareness of our own sin. Hence Paul could preach against homosexuality as a sin, because he had himself confessed freely, "I don't do the good I want to do; instead, I do the evil that I do not want to do. . . . What an unhappy man I am! Who will rescue me from this body that is taking me to death?" (Rom. 7:19, 24).

The conservative witness, however, seems more anxious to proclaim itself "the Moral Majority" than other fellow sinners. Thus, it bears no saving power for homosexuals, but often provokes their scornful rejection instead.

But neither do the liberals take seriously our universal human condition of sin, our innate tendency to make decisions based on our self-centered desires rather than on God's will for us. In fact, to celebrate a homosexual's "free choice" is as counterproductive as to condemn it. For a little boy simply does not have "free choice" regarding the emotion of his parents or the inherent ungodliness of the world into which he is born. He can only submit to his family and to society—until he discovers that Jesus has come into the world, *his* world, that he might be born again into the family of God and His society/kingdom.

The homosexual, meanwhile, may declare, "What I'm doing can't be a sin, because I was born this way!" Yet the biblical faith understands that all of us are born into sin, and are unable by our own natural power to fulfill God's will for our lives. The Good News of our faith is precisely that the inborn brokenness of our human nature has been overcome and redeemed by Jesus, that the power to walk in His victory is accessible to those who surrender their lives to Him. God holds us accountable, therefore, not for the worldly circumstances of our "first," natural human birth, but indeed, for our willingness to meet Jesus in death at the Cross and there receive a "second," spiritual birth. Jesus Himself underscored this distinction: "A person is born physically of human parents, but he is born spiritually of the Spirit" (John 3:6).

It is not a sin to be born of a possessive mother and a distant father, nor to have consequent homosexual fantasies. It is a sin to refuse to surrender yourself to Jesus and let God begin to shape you into His image as a man. Granted, to do so may be extremely difficult for some men, depending on the intensity of the mother's clinging and the father's absence. But Jesus never promised that His way would be easy. Dying to one's natural self is hard; Jesus Himself begged that such a cup might be taken from Him. But He did not run from the Lion.

Homosexuals are quick to charge their critics with "homophobia" (fear of homosexuality)—and in fact, they are largely justified in doing so. For the vast majority of us males in our father-starved culture justly fear a mis-focused attraction to other men. To bring a prophetic word against homosexuality, one must confess this at the Cross, this longing for true and appropriate manly affection, and let Jesus lead him to the Father for healing—not hide it behind an aggressive antihomosexual stance.

All of us men, regardless of our sexual actions, must sooner or later face the sword of God's truth as it "judges the desires and thoughts of man's heart" (Heb. 4:12b). Only so far as we face and submit to that sword are we licensed to wield it ourselves. If the conservatives' sin is that they have fancied themselves more judging than God, the liberals' sin is that they have fancied that they could be "more kind than God's law."[3] As a conservative, the surgeon curses the patient and slashes him ruthlessly; as a liberal, he glibly pronounces the patient "healthy" simply to spare him the pain of surgery, however necessary.

Declaring homosexuality to be "healthy" is therefore a quick-fix verbal cosmetic which may get fathers off the hook temporarily and save the son from the difficult work of looking honestly at himself. But men today who are distraught by sexual feelings for other men do not need to be told they are healthy, any more than they need to be damned to hell.

They need to be told that their Father God loves them, and has come in Jesus Christ to set them free to be true men of the Father. Clearly, this cannot be done with integrity by Christian men who hurl judgment while hiding behind what "the Bible says," and refusing to face and surrender to Jesus their own longing for fatherly love.

At the same time, no Christian therapist dares to pretend that overcoming homosexuality is easy. But in Jesus, God did not promise us an easy road; the resurrection requires the Cross. In fact, I am convinced that the American Psychiatric Society removed homosexuality from its list of mental illnesses simply because the psychiatrists were tired of failing in their human efforts to heal it.

If the American Medical Association were to give up on finding a cure for cancer and tomorrow declare that cancer is no longer an illness, it would become an instant target of rage and ridicule. Yet when the psychiatrists do just that with homosexuality, society cheers. Why? Primarily because we are a lazy, self-centered species which labors to avoid honest self-examination, and applauds anyone who would save us from it. Those who are too well educated to urge that homosexuals be quarantined, sanitize their fear and denial by smugly declaring that the whole issue should not be a concern.

At an even deeper level, however, we are simply blinded by our myopic Western scientific materialism, which proudly refuses to recognize spiritual reality—and thus cannot recognize spiritual disease.

Any doctor understands that diagnosis is the primary step toward treatment and cure. Even cancer, for example, can proceed with its deadly effects long before the patient is aware of its presence; that is why regular checkups are urged. Early diagnosis is key; not to recognize the disease is to capitulate to its deadly purpose.

Nevertheless, some people do not get regular checkups, nor do they go to the doctor even when they feel discomfort. Why? Because they do not want to face the truth. Rather than face the reality of their illness and do what needs to be done for healing, they live in the fantasy of the lie—and they die.

Similarly, people who recognize spiritual reality and the God who oversees it will be concerned for their spiritual welfare. They will seek regular checkups by praying, asking God to show them where they might have missed the mark He has set. They will enjoy fellowship with other believers who can help them see themselves more honestly. As the psalmist proclaimed, "No one can see his own errors; deliver me, Lord, from hidden faults" (19:12).

Official acceptance of homosexuality, therefore, is just another example of how men have withdrawn from the manly sword of truth. Offered as a gesture of mercy and help, this acceptance is, in fact, profoundly irresponsible from a spiritual perspective, for it abandons the distraught male in his predicament and closes the door on his hope for healing.

From a spiritual perspective, homosexuality reflects a deep inner brokenness which only the Father God can heal. Contrary to its physical expression, it represents not a physical closeness to other males, but a profound physical alienation rooted in the absence of fatherly affection and bonding. To recognize homosexuality as a spiritual illness—a sin—does not make homosexuals any worse than other men in God's sight. As Paul noted, ". . . there is no difference at all: everyone has sinned and is far away from God's saving presence" (Rom. 3:22). Homosexual acts simply make one a candidate for God's healing, along with the rest of us sinners. For so Paul concludes, "But by the free gift of God's grace all are put right with him through Christ Jesus, who sets them free" (v. 23).

Not long ago, alcoholism was seen as incurable. No one could come up with a way to overcome it that could be replicated by others. Society condemned alcoholics, and hid them. Then Bill W. testified that he was recovering from alcoholism through a twelve-step program that was explicitly and deliberately "spiritual," though "not religious." Through the consequent worldwide ministry of Alcoholics Anonymous, hundreds of thousands of alcoholics have found freedom from their addiction.

What if the AMA had restrained Bill W. and told him, "You don't need a spiritual perspective on your life; you don't even need to worry about your drinking any more, because we have declared that alcoholism is no longer a disorder"?

Until relatively recently, few homosexual men could testify to any way of changing their orientation. Churches, even as they condemned homosexuals, could not mediate the power necessary to bring lasting change. Today, however, more and more men are emerging with convincing testimonies that they have indeed been turned around by yielding to the Father God's love through Jesus Christ. Recognizing the spiritual root of the problem, as with alcoholism, is forcing us to reexamine our earlier, secularly guided conclusions.

As Rita Bennett notes in her book, *How to Pray for Inner Healing,*

> Many claim that (homosexuality) can be hereditary, and therefore not only incurable, but a "valid life-style." I do not wish to pass judgment on this or any other human problem, but the persons I have prayed with had clearly been programmed to it by past hurts, and these were healed.[4]

Desert Stream, a ministry in Santa Monica, California, "for homosexuals who seek to be new creatures in Christ," is one Christian program today that witnesses to many such transformed lives. Director Andy Comiskey, for example, writes in a newsletter article titled, "Healing the Child Within," about

> . . . the child within myself, that part of me which sought from day one, and continues to seek, love and affirmation from others. My child's journey has been a confusing one, in part due to its needy attempt to find love and identity in sexual relationships with men.[5]

Lamenting "our 'Christian' tendency" to "interpret that child within as 'of the flesh,' and sinfully needy"—and then our tendency "to shut the child up and treat him as an enemy," Comiskey notes that,

> Our efforts to suppress that child are doomed to failure. For that part of ourself which has never grown up has at its core some legitimate needs for which God has compassion, as well as a desire to meet those needs constructively.[6]

In particular, Comiskey declares that a child needs "affirming relationships with the same sex, especially with the same-sex parent" in order to secure "self-worth and clear sense of gender." That is,

> In joining with the same-sex erotically, the needy child within seeks in adult form the affirmation and emotional intimacy from the same-sex that was never properly attained in childhood.[7]

He notes that the majority of his clients therefore

> attest to the fact that gay sex wasn't really the motivating factor in their homosexual pursuits, while same-sex intimacy was, (and therefore reflected) an emotional need as opposed to an erotic one.[8]

Comiskey then offers three basic steps to "remedy the destructive behavior of the inner child, and his adversary, the critical parent." First, unlike orthodox conservatism,

> We must accept the reality of our homosexual feelings. Remember that refusing to listen to the cries of the inner child will only increase his voice.[9]

Second,

> In order to accept the child, the critical parent must be replaced by a more kindly source. The only way I know of effectively silencing the critical parent is to receive in faith the affirming voice of our heavenly Father, who breaks through our own paltry system of perfection and its counterpart of condemnation to reveal His patient, all-knowing, all-loving concern.[10]

Third, unlike orthodox liberalism, one must learn to "set limits" on one's "needy and compulsive tendencies" because,

> Your inner child will only be further abused, and all the more needy, if you indulge him in homosexual activity. Firmly and patiently setting limits provides the forum in which his real needs can emerge and be met.[11]

Other Christian writers reflect a similar understanding of the roots of homosexuality and portray its healing through prayer.

Ruth Carter Stapleton, in her 1976 book, *The Gift of Inner Healing*, records her counseling with a young man named Jody. After pouring out his anguish about his homosexual orientation, he told her his story. Stapleton notes:

> It was as I expected. His father had died when he was eight, and his mother had never remarried. During the period of time between ages nine and fourteen, when he normally would have shifted his interest and affection from his mother to his father, he had no father to whom he could shift his attentions.
>
> In normal emotional development, when a boy reaches the age of thirteen to sixteen, he begins to take an interest in girls again and shifts from the masculine attraction back to the feminine. Since this period of development was absent in Jody, it was obvious why men interested him more than women. His deep mind was still reaching out for a man, a father, that male affection God intended him to have, free from the overt sexual drive he now knew.[12]

Stapleton then prayed with Jody by inviting Jesus to move into the masculine gap and be his father; the prayers included Jody's seeing Jesus and himself playing baseball together, as a father and son might do.

She then adds that, of course, not all homosexuals have deceased fathers, as Jody did:

> Some young men need to be healed of the image of the strong overcontrolling mother who gave the child a confused sense of

manhood. Every person is different, and only by discernment, divine knowledge, and the guidance of the Holy Spirit can one know how to pray.[13]

In her book, *Emotionally Free,* Rita Bennett portrays Dave, who at age eleven was sexually assaulted by several boys. When she asked him to remember the scene and invite Jesus into it, he balked: "I feel so unclean I don't think I can go to Him." With Bennett's encouragement, he eventually agreed:

> Dave visualized his eleven-year-old child-self going to Jesus. As he saw Jesus receive him with love, tears began to roll down his face. He was able to tell the boys who had abused him that he forgave them and set them free—and himself, too. He asked God to forgive him for any willing participation on his part.[14]

A deeper root of Dave's problem, however, was yet to be revealed. As they continued praying, he remembered a recurrent nightmare which had no clear focus. Eventually, the Holy Spirit showed him a mental picture of himself in his mother's womb, and his father—an alcoholic with a violent temper—trying to kill him by beating on his mother's stomach.

For several minutes, Dave cried out his pent-up pain from that experience, which his natural mind could not have recalled. Bennett then prayed about Dave's birth, as Dave exclaimed, "I don't want to be born! I want to die!" He was reflecting his father's death wish for him, and his mother's fear of having him because of her husband's anger. Bennett then encouraged Dave to see Jesus there in the delivery room as he was being born:

> "Jesus is there with the doctor, and everything is going to be just fine. Whether anyone else wanted you then or not, Jesus did. He is delighted you are being born because He knows you're going to become a child of God. Feel his arms holding you. He's proud of you. You're just what He wanted!" As he saw Jesus with him, receiving him, rejoicing over him, Dave's weeping ceased completely, and he relaxed.[15]

Eventually, through further prayer, Dave tells his father in the presence of Jesus that he forgives him for not wanting him, and for trying to kill him before he was born.

Three years later, Dave called Bennett to express his joy and appreciation:

> "I've had a great deal of healing from homosexual thought patterns, and I feel a growing release from them. Do you think my feelings toward men could have been because I was looking for my father's love?"
>
> "I believe that's true," I replied. "You were programmed to feel rejection from your father before birth. Growing up, you experienced the same thing."[16]

Similarly, Leanne Payne in her *Crisis in Masculinity* tells of Richard, "addicted to pornography and homosexuality," and the son of an alcoholic father and self-centered mother. His basic problem, Payne declares, was not "that he was 'homosexual:'"

> Rather, his problem consisted in the fact that he was split off from his masculinity and as a consequence from his real self.[17]

That is,

> He was separated from the power to see and accept himself *as a man*. (italics added)[18]

As Payne listens to Richard's story, she notes that it

> . . . became very clear . . . that his feelings of being "castrated, emasculated, weak, queer, twisted" were continually strengthened by the father who remained distant and by the mother who, when functioning at all, pampered him to the extreme. To her, he was a helpless, hurting appendage of herself, a self that was narcissistic, depressed, and utterly passive.[19]

Significantly, in his homosexual lovers and fantasies, Richard sought partners who seemed bold, muscular, tough, reflecting the common pattern in homosexuals that,

. . . what they admire in the other man will be their own unaffirmed characteristics, those from which they are separated, can in no way see, and therefore cannot accept as part of their own being. These attributes they have projected onto another person.[20]

This being separated from one's masculinity because it was not affirmed by the father has profound consequences for the adult male:

To one degree or another, countless men share with Richard this painful inner story. One may act it out as a Don Juan, a compulsive seducer of women; another may live as a compulsive liar and boaster in order to prove himself; a third may chronically fear to step out and lead as he is gifted to lead, to speak the truth or act the truth as it is called for. Yet another may simply be caught in the mire of an uncreative, passive loneliness. He will suffer from a sensitive but overly developed feminine side. All, unaffirmed in their masculinity, are trapped in their own failure to accept themselves. All are in turn unable adequately to affirm offspring in their sexual and personal identities.[21]

Yet the consequences of a wounded masculinity, Payne points out, are not limited to the men, themselves:

Unaffirmed men are unable adequately to affirm their own sons and daughters as male and female and therefore as persons. Until men are once again functioning in this vital capacity, women will continue to attempt to fill the gap in vain, and will continue to verbalize their pain and confusion.[22]

One thinks immediately of the "pain and confusion" described by the increasing number of feminist writers now calling for more strength and initiative from men, as noted in chapter 12. As Payne concludes,

When men are healed, the healing of women will naturally follow.[23]

Where, then, does a man turn today for that healing? If, as Payne declares, the "key" to healing the masculine soul "lies in the love and affirmation of a whole father," and if, in fact, the mother cannot bridge the gap left by a missing father, "no matter how whole [she] is psychologically and spiritually," what can an unaffirmed man do whose father was and is "missing," either physically or emotionally?

The women themselves, despite their cresting sense of self-assertiveness and strength, are beginning to realize that they cannot provide that essential masculine affirmation for their husbands and lovers any more than for their sons. Too often, meanwhile, the man today has been turning to the woman and expecting her to give it to him, because in his fear of manhood, as personified by the absent father, he has concluded that such affirmation is not available from men.

When a man asks his woman for something that only another man can give him, two ingredients are necessary for healing. First, the woman must be strong enough to resist the man's demands and not let either her natural sense of compassion or her engendered fear of rejection lead her to "mother" him. Second, the man must begin to trust in the Father God's power to call forth his masculine strength; he must submit his inner wounds to the sword of truth and the Father God's healing embrace.

Women, for the past ten or twenty years, have been equipping themselves better and better for their own part. It's time we men began to do ours.

8
Warrior Redeemed

IN A 1987 SUNDAY *Doonesbury* strip, cartoonist Garry Trudeau pictures Joanie Caucus and married daughter Joan, Jr., discussing the effects of war toys on male child development—and in particular, on Joanie's five-year-old boy.

"I gave him some paints for Christmas, and a kitchen, and a doctor's kit, and a little clown to be his patient," the boy's mother declares.

> He wanted guns, of course, but I've decided I'm just not going to put up with war toys. I can't help thinking that one of the reasons little boys act so aggressive is that their parents are constantly arming them to the teeth.[1]

Suddenly, from beneath the table where the two women are talking, the boy leaps up wearing a kitchen pot as a helmet and brandishing a clown doll as a rifle. Extending the doll's arm as a barrel, he points it at Joanie and shouts, "BUDDA, BUDDA, BUDDA, BUDDA! BLAM! You're dead! You're DEAD, SHE-RA!"

As the doll's hand smokes, Joanie looks at her daughter in dismay and reflects on her earlier pronouncement: "Just a theory, of course."[1]

Theories aside, few of us men today cannot recall fun times "playing war" with friends as boys. As a "war baby" myself, born in 1944, I redeemed many a rainy day playing with little brown metal soldiers perched atop clocks, chairs, and couch pillows. Playmates would draw "men" one turn at a time from the box, and the prone sharpshooters always went first, since you could hide them better.

Outdoors, one of our favorite neighborhood games was for each boy to take a turn racing across the yard while the rest crouched or lay down holding imaginary rifles, pointed at the runner. At a signal, all would shout out sounds of gunfire—some machine-gun staccato, others single shots—and the runner would be obliged to fall. The game was simply to see who could fall the most dramatically. Occasionally, after tumbling with great flurry and shouts of anguish, a boy might try to get up again as if only wounded—prompting a renewed burst of gunfire from the rest of us and another opportunity for an even more graphic "death." Not uncommonly, cheers would follow such a performance.

At age eleven, I joined a Boy Scout "patrol" and learned with the other boys how to march in military drills, fire a rifle, send coded messages, and the like. From the TV series *Victory at Sea* to John Wayne war movies to *Life* magazine pictures, war images and stories fascinated me; my boy's mind could only imagine war as a glorious adventure in manhood.

True, the media's war images were framed with the understanding that such activity as war is dirty and awful and so, to be avoided. Yet, if the truth be told, that hint of the forbidden was to me more of an attraction than a diversion. Indeed, the very dirtiness of it all seemed to beckon me, just as Mother's insistence on clean hands dismayed me.

While war's graphic images of destruction initially held my

attention, eventually my focus shifted from war, itself, to the particularly admirable character qualities which were required in battle and demonstrated by the men who participated in it. The term "war hero" entered my vocabulary at an early age, and I wanted, along with my friends, to emulate such an image.

From my limited boyhood perspective, however, I could not distinguish between the awful nature of warmaking itself and the war hero. Thus in some sense, war became associated in my mind with the admirable war hero. Whatever negative reality war might engender, it became for me a preeminent context for demonstrating a rich variety of the character traits essential to manhood.

At some later point in my development, I passed beyond simply admiring the war hero to desiring a war in which I, too, might demonstrate those manly traits. True, at some deeper level the thought of it frightened me. But even that fear was more an encouragement than a deterrent; after all, unless an act is fearful, no one can recognize it as requiring courage.

With a mixture of disappointment and relief, I found myself coming into puberty too late for the Korean War, and wondering whether I might ever have the opportunity to prove my manliness in war. In college, I applied for Naval ROTC and, to my great disappointment, was rejected for color blindness. My college was in North Carolina, where the early civil rights sit-ins began, and by the time I graduated, I felt a deep sympathy for black people in their struggle. On the horizon, the Vietnam War was escalating, and my draft board beckoned; but I decided instead to go to Africa as a Peace Corps volunteer.

On returning from Nigeria, I flirted with the Army, going far enough in the application process to be offered a commission and orders to report for missile-launch training at Ft. Huachuca, Arizona. But by this time, the peace movement had won my allegiance so sufficiently that I secured a deferment, and instead taught junior high school in the inner city until becoming twenty-six and thus ineligible for the draft.

Twenty years later, I can remember clearly the sense I had back then that staying out of the military was best for me at the time. And yet, while I had effectively outgrown my boyhood perception of war, nevertheless something required of manhood seemed to have been bypassed, overlooked, even dodged. Try as I might to scoff and convince myself that my active decision "for peace and not war" made me more authentically a man, such a conviction never penetrated beyond my intellect into my heart.

Confused and frustrated, I knew that manhood required the warrior. But it never occurred to me to ask, "Can the warrior exist without killing and destruction?" any more than "Can the sword heal?"

To my delight, if not relief, I found this part of myself portrayed by Robert Bly. At the outset, Bly refers to the fifties male as,

> . . . hard-working, responsible, fairly well disciplined: he didn't see women's souls very well, though he looked at their bodies a lot. . . . (He) was vulnerable to collective opinion: if you were a man, you were supposed to like football games, be aggressive, stick up for the United States, never cry, and always provide. But this image of the male lacked feminine space. . . . It lacked compassion, in a way that led directly to the unbalanced pursuit of the Vietnam war. . . .[2]

Concluding that "the '50s male had a clear vision of what a man is," Bly then notes that,

> . . . during the '60s, another sort of male appeared. The waste and anguish of the Vietnam war made men question what an adult male really is. And the women's movement encouraged men to actually *look* at women, forcing them to . . . see their own feminine side and pay attention to it.[3]

Yet in that basically good and essential process of growth, we men became "soft males," with no "life-giving energy." Having rejected the most accessible model of male strength, namely warmaking, we essentially abdicated that strength to the women and concentrated on being gentler ourselves.

Thus Bly recalls the bumper sticker of that era urging men to resist the draft: "WOMEN SAY YES TO MEN WHO SAY NO":

> (T)he women were definitely saying that they preferred the softer receptive male. . . . So the development of men was disturbed a little there: nonreceptive maleness was equated with violence, and receptivity was rewarded.[4]

Indeed, from this perspective, one might say that the man, having bonded to the feminist movement and its values, became trapped. That is, lacking Bly's "deeper masculine" model, the emotionally whole father who could call him away from the mother/woman, the man could not integrate this new feminine part of himself and move beyond it into real masculine polarity.

Women scorned the warrior, and we followed suit. Bly notes that a little boy at home learns to view his father through his mother's eyes—and judge him accordingly. Thus we viewed our masculinity inappropriately, through the women's eyes.

Something essential, we knew, was missing in our wholesale rejection of the warrior.

But what?

Esquire magazine's contributing editor and former World War II pilot George Leonard answers that question as he laments the current state of the warrior image in American culture. He rejects Rambo not simply because he commits violence, but because he exhibits few traits applicable to daily civilian life. Instead, Rambo portrays the warrior as,

> . . . an American revenge fantasy, a vivid dream image of single-minded, unrestrained action that would somehow erase the frustrations of Vietnam, Iran, and Lebanon, and set things right in one miraculous catharsis of blood and gore.[5]

Seeking a more enduring, adaptable warrior image, Leonard asks, "Is there some way that the warrior spirit at its best and highest can contribute to a lasting peace and to the quality of our individual lives during the time of peace?"[6]

Rather than idolize the warrior, as do the hawks of orthodox conservatism, or condemn him, as do the doves of orthodox liberalism, Leonard would redeem him by identifying and distilling his finest attributes down to character traits which all of us might use to overcome the struggles of our daily lives. Leonard seeks a path for those men today who cannot abide the reckless violence of Rambo or the equally reckless passivity of one who neither resists evil nor strives for victory.

Leonard asks a group of Army Green Berets how they define "the ideal warrior":

> They cited loyalty, patience, intensity, calmness, compassion and will. They agreed that the true warrior knows himself, knows his limitations. . . . Self-mastery, according to the Special Forces men, is a warrior's central motivation. He is always practicing, always seeking to hone his skills, so as to become the best possible instrument for accomplishing his mission. The warrior takes calculated risks and tests himself repeatedly. He believes in something greater than himself: a religion, a cause. He does not worship violence, but is at home with it. He may snivel (their word for complain), but he is not a victim.[7]

In fact, some of those interviewed "felt that the warrior could exist even outside the military." This impressed Leonard "with the importance these elite soldiers placed on service and protection."

The true warrior criterion for us men today is neither the body count hailed by conservatives nor the "sanctity of life" proclaimed by liberals; it is instead a deliberate lifestyle. The issue of one's manhood focuses neither on the question, "How many men did you kill?" nor "How often did you refuse to fight?" Instead, we need to appraise ourselves according to several specific character traits, as in the following questions:

- When have you demonstrated loyalty to someone or some cause greater than yourself?
- When have you shown patience during trial, disciplined intensity in a task, calmness "under fire"?
- What skills are you working to hone?
- When have you taken a calculated risk and tested yourself?
- When have you taken initiative to right a wrong?

- When have you demonstrated compassion by taking action in behalf of another person?

Clearly, war not only offers ready opportunity for all these traits, it fosters circumstances which demand them. In a footnote citing World War II combat veteran and philosopher J. Glenn Gray's book, *The Warriors*, Leonard notes "war's terrible and enduring appeal: the opportunity to yield to destructive impulses, to sacrifice for others, to live vividly in the moment."[8]

He concludes: "The appeal of war is not a popular subject, but until we deal with it openly and undogmatically we may never find a warrior's path toward peace."[9]

If indeed the warrior spirit is intrinsic to males, then efforts to eliminate the warrior image are intrinsically emasculating. The more productive path toward peacemaking is the one Leonard advocates and describes as, "a way of living that would provide the challenges of combat without its horrors":

> We need passion. We need challenge and risk. We need to be pushed to our limits. And I believe this is just what happens when we accept a warrior's code, when we try to live each moment as a warrior, whether in education, job, marriage, child rearing, or recreation. The truth is that we don't have to go to combat to go to war. Life is fired at us like a bullet, and there is no escaping it short of death. All escape attempts—drugs, aimless travel, the distractions of the media, empty material pursuits—are sure to fail in the long run, as more and more of us are beginning to learn.[10]

Significantly, in seeking the ultimate context for the "warrior spirit," Leonard finds the secular vocabulary inadequate. He wonders, as Gray does, "whether a peaceful society can be made attractive enough to wean men away from the appeals of battle." Quoting Gray, Leonard looks beyond efforts "to eliminate the social, economic, and political injustices that are always the immediate occasion of hostilities." For indeed, even if these goals should be accomplished,

> we shall be confronted with the spiritual emptiness and inner hunger that impel many men toward combat. Our society has not

begun to wrestle with this problem of how to provide fulfillment to human life, to which war is so often an illusory path.[11]

The concern for peacemakers is therefore not that men go to war and destroy, but that we have not fostered creative and productive occasions for men to demonstrate the essential qualities of manhood. What if, indeed, soldiers really do hate war, but in the absence of peaceful alternatives to manhood, prefer it to denying and squelching their true, manly self? If so, then all of us are to be held accountable for not diligently seeking such alternatives.

Being gentle, expressing feelings, caring for children, and demonstrating other "feminine" parts of ourselves, while helpful and important, simply cannot supplant the essential masculine character traits as goals. This was evident in the sixties when we pursued a false syllogism: men are violent; thus, to make males not violent, we must remove their masculinity and make them more feminine. Now we are learning instead to encourage the deeper masculine traits which, when otherwise focused do not need to seek violence.

Certainly, competitive team sports have been the most readily accessible alternative to warmaking for developing these masculine traits.

Some years ago, I was amazed to see a striking and graphic portrayal of this phenomenon on the cover of a Marvel comic book, "Sgt. Fury and His Howling Commandos."[12] Two caricatures of the same individual leap across the page superimposed on one another, their limbs and bodies literally parallel. With fierce and angry faces, each has one arm extended straight out from the shoulder, the other cocked to throw. One holds a football and wears a football helmet and uniform; the other holds a hand grenade and wears an army helmet and uniform. The title/caption, printed on a series of collegiate banners, reads, "FROM THE/CAMPUS GRIDIRON/ TO THE BLAZING BATTLEFRONT/THE NEWEST HOWLER IS/THE ALL-AMERICAN!

A background insert pictures several Nazi-helmeted soldiers sprawled on the ground, and ahead of them eight men carrying machine guns advance, led by a larger man with a larger, smoking gun—clearly Sgt. Fury.

I showed this portrait to my "For Men Only" class and invited them to list the virtues represented in it. Reviewing their composite list, we found no virtue exclusive to either caricature. All applied to both soldier and sportsman:

courage/daring
righteousness
camaraderie/fellowship
discipline
determination
strength
action/energy
glory/approbation
anger rightly focused
enemy/opponent overcome

At this point, the Christian might ask how the Church can begin to foster such values and provide opportunities for men to act them out. We dare not consider such a question, however, until we have asked the fundamental question, "Does Jesus exhibit the character traits of the "ideal warrior"?

The Gospel accounts reveal Jesus' courage, in returning to Jerusalem, where He knew the religious authorities wanted to eliminate Him; His righteousness, in turning from Satan's temptations; His fellowship, with the disciples; His discipline, in early morning prayer; His determination, even when rejected at His hometown; His strength, in casting out demons; His energy, in calling forth Lazarus from the tomb; His glory, in being baptized with the Father's blessing; His anger, against the temple money-changers; and His overcoming the enemy, in meeting death and rising victorious.

And Jesus never killed anyone, nor destroyed anything.

In fact, Jesus is the authentic warrior, in whom God has given us power to battle victoriously the struggles of this world.

Furthermore, the early Church drew explicit battle images to describe its nature and calling.

Note the apostle's encouragement to the Ephesians:

Finally, build up your strength in union with the Lord and by means of his mighty power. Put on all the armor that God gives you, so that you will be able to stand up against the Devil's evil tricks. For we are not fighting against human beings but against the wicked spiritual forces in the heavenly world, the rulers, authorities, and cosmic powers of this dark age. So put on God's armor now! Then when the evil day comes, you will be able to resist the enemy's attacks; and after fighting to the end, you will still hold your ground (Eph. 6:10–13).

To our Christian forebears, commitment to the faith began not with a decision to enter the struggles of the world, but rather, with awareness that all of us are already in the midst of a fierce and momentous spiritual battle in a world that is under siege by God's spiritual enemy Satan and his forces. We have no choice about becoming a part of the battle, but only whether we shall fight on the Lord's side or be overcome by the enemy.

During the 1987 NBA playoffs, Los Angeles Laker forward A.C. Green was featured in a sports-page interview headlined, "A.C. plugs religion into his successful career."[13] When he was asked, "How do you reconcile your religious beliefs with the fact that you play a rough sport that at times can turn even violent?" Green replied:

God wants His people to be warriors—to be battlers and fighters. And I don't mean waging warfare, or getting into fights. What I mean is being a battler and fighter in doing as well as you can in your chosen profession. I don't think any Christian should be a passive kind of person. If he is, then he's going to be headed for a lot of problems in his spiritual walk.

Significantly, Green distinguishes between physical violence and the "spirit of might" which God requires of His people:

I'm ready to battle when I step on a court. I expect to fight—not a physical fight when people exchange punches—but a fight to get rebounds and to score points. Just look at God's warriors in the Bible—they were always ready to fight, destroy their enemies and possess their land. It's that spirit of might that moves me. I don't start anything, but I won't back down from anybody, either.

Green affirmed the discipline necessary in order to become such a warrior. A year earlier, he was not even used in the Lakers playoff series; in 1987 he was a valuable starter. Declaring that "the God I serve performs miracles," he also explained that our own human efforts are an essential part of becoming what God wants for us:

> In the New Testament in the book of Galatians, there is a saying, "That which a man sows is what he shall reap." What that means is that if you're willing to put your time into something, you'll get something out of it. And during the last off-season, I was determined to become as good as I can at playing basketball. I talked to people like Pat Riley (Lakers coach) and Jerry West—and listened to what they had to say. I played hard in the summer league and worked hard on improving my foul shooting and rebounding techniques. And all the work has paid off.

Hence, when Jesus promised that He would send the Holy Spirit to the believers as "the Helper," the text uses the Greek word *paraclete*, which, as John Sandford has explained,[14] is an ancient warrior's term. Greek soldiers, went into battle in pairs, so when the enemy attacked they could draw together back-to-back, covering each other's blindside. One's battle partner was the *paraclete*. Today the Holy Spirit comes to cover our blindside (the spiritual reality unperceived by our human senses and rational minds) when the spiritual enemy attacks. As the battle partner, the Holy Spirit brings to the believer such essential gifts/weapons as supernatural knowledge, wisdom, and discernment (1 Cor. 12:8, 10).

The early Church's understanding of sacraments also was war-related, based on the original meaning of the Latin *sacramentum*, defined by Webster as "in ancient Rome, the military oath taken by every Roman soldier, pledging him to obey his commander, and not to desert his standard."[15]

Our Christian forebears therefore saw Jesus as the commander-in-chief of God's army not only in Heaven, but in this world (see Joshua 5:13–15 and Rev. 19:11–21). The standard of Jesus, lifted high above His forces, is of course the cross, before which all are revealed as sinners, upon which the power of sin was broken, and through which the enemy's grip on God's people was loosed once and for all.

So the sacraments—especially the eucharist—were seen by the early Church as occasions for believers to reenlist in God's forces and reassume the humility of loyalty and disciplined obedience. Even the protestant reformers held this high estimation of the sacraments, and would be appalled to see how we protestants today take them so lightly. As Calvin declared, "Whoever abstains voluntarily from the practice of the sacraments, thinking that he does not need them, scorns Christ, rejects his grace, and snuffs out his Holy Spirit."[16]

A pastor friend, who entered the military at a young age, became a believer years later and a minister only after his twenty-year retirement, noted the significant parallels between his military induction and Christian commitment. All citizens, he pointed out, say the Pledge of Allegiance as a sort of "philosophical agreement." But to become a soldier, you must take the Oath of Allegiance to the Constitution, which requires your willingness to "defend" the nation by sacrificing your life for it.

This action, he declared, represents "a cleavage with the past, a transition to a new group," one more narrowly defined, more risky: "Certainly, you hope that you won't have to die in battle, but you'd be foolish to think you'd never be called to." Clearly, such a commitment places the soldier above the average citizen, who ostensibly concerns himself most intently with self-preservation, that is, with fulfilling his own, self-centered desires and needs.

"When I became a Christian," my friend declared, "all these apparently military issues were called forth in me:

Before, I'd gone to church, like so many who pledge their allegiance to God, as if to say no more than "Yes, we agree God is OK." But when I stood up, went forward, and gave my life to Christ, it was a different story, a real and life-changing commitment for me. Sure, I didn't want to suffer for my belief in Him, but I knew it'd be foolish for me to think I never would.

This redeemed image of the warrior and his calling brings into question the typical, mainline church's approach to men. Most often, we draw back from challenging men to greater commitment, assuming their laziness. We then wonder why men have so little respect for the church—even as we presume so little respect for them. But what if we told men up front that to join the church of Jesus Christ is, like the ancient "sacramentum," to enlist in God's army and to place their lives on the line? This approach would be based on the warrior spirit in every man, and so would offer the greatest hope for restoring authentic Christian manhood to the Body of Christ.

To be sure, it would be risky: what if the lazy men didn't come?

But what if the real men did?

9

Boots for a Working Man

SHORTLY AFTER I LEFT the parish ministry to write full-time, a pair of cowboy boots beckoned to me from a newspaper sale ad. Standing tall, pointing to the football scoreboard, the boots stirred within me the thrill of seeing Hopalong Cassidy leap onto his white horse in one powerful move, thrusting the point of his boot into the stirrup to mount up.

Gazing at the ad, I remembered buying spurs at the dime store with my allowance and fixing them to my Stride Rite oxfords so they would catch the floor just right and jingle as I strode fearlessly down the hallway. Never mind Mother's scolding for scratching her hardwood floors; a cowboy does what he has to do.

Boyhood fancies. . . .

Still, I had never owned a pair of cowboy boots; nor, if the truth be told, had I ever so much as tried any on. . . .

The very name of the store—Thieves Market—hinted at

forbidden mysteries of manhood; and in the spirit of new freedom I now felt in working for myself, I decided to see if cowboy boots might be right for me after all.

As I entered the store, an imposing fellow in a large, broad-brimmed Stetson and shiny black tooled boots approached me.

"C'n ah he'p y'?" he offered amicably, thumb-hooking his belt.

At once it occurred to me that without his hat and boots, the man would have been as much as a foot shorter.

"Well. . . ," I began hesitantly, "I was just looking for . . . some boots."

"Waal, y'come to the rat place," he announced, chuckling and gesturing broadly around the store. "What sort was ya lookin' fer?"

I paused uneasily, following his gesture and glancing at the racks of boots on all sides of us. White, black, brown, tan, swirled, branded, stitched, tooled—they pointed at me. "Oh," I said quickly, hoping not to betray my ignorance, "I thought maybe . . . uh. . . ." To my dismay, I stopped mid-sentence. Indeed, what kind of boots *was* I looking for? I hadn't realized they came in so many styles. All at once, it struck me. "Something not so shiny!" I blurted out—then catching myself as I glanced at his glistening feet. "I mean . . . you know—something with a sort of natural finish."

"Rat ovuh hee-uh," he declared, turning and leading me to a small rack toward the back of the store.

Now that's more like it, I thought. Rubber soles, unpolished. "These look good," I said, checking the labels and drawing a pair my size off the rack.

"Them's workin' boots," he noted as I pulled at the leather loops. To my surprise, the boot slipped right on and fit nicely.

"Them kind got rubber soles that hold real good," he added.

Straining to appear casual, as if I put on boots every morning of my life, I nodded and then, with both now securely on my feet, I leaned forward from my stool. *Here goes*, I thought. Smiling quickly, I eased upward . . . and stood right there, in my cowboy boots!

"Them kind'r good fer most eny kinda work," the salesman was saying. "Don' matter if yer drivin' a truck or bulldozer or what-ivvir."

Again I smiled quickly and nodded. Then slowly, I stepped forward. Not bad, I thought. Surprisingly comfortable! Soon I was striding up and down the carpet, my thumb hooked in my belt.

"What kinda work y' do, enyhow?" he was asking. "You drive a truck or sompthin'?"

Startled, I stopped mid-stride. "W-what?"

"Y' work construction, mebbe, outderrs, fer boots like them?"

"Uh . . . well," I said quickly, then paused. In a flash I ruled out the truth. Minister? Impossible. Writer? No way. Not for these boots. "That is . . . I mean, actually, I'm not working just now," I said finally.

"Waal, whativvir y' do, them boots'll do'y fine," he said matter-of-factly, then turned as another customer, burly and sun-burned, drew close.

My eyes dropped to my feet, natural leather finish and all.

"Ah'll be rat hee-uh if y'need me," he said.

"Oh . . . thanks," I murmured, looking up as his shiny black boots turned away from me.

Standing there alone in my cowboy boots, I sighed and un-hooked my thumbs. Maybe they were a little uncomfortable after all, at the top where they rubbed a bit against my calf. Gingerly, I stepped over the stool and sat down.

Again, I sighed. And then quickly, I grasped the heel of the boot and pulled.

The boots incident occurred in my forty-second year, and as I have shared it with other fellow professional men, I have met with universal identification. "I was with you every 'step' of the way," one minister friend responded.

I am convinced that much of the inner conflict which I and other educated men today experience with respect to our jobs and our manhood is rooted in our history. Most of us are not more than two or three generations away from the so-called "working class." Our "class" today no longer bears the term "working." We are therefore caught between an image of our physically hard-working grandfathers in farms and factories, and the white-collar professional in his antiseptic office building.

Our culture, meanwhile, clearly attributes greater masculinity to the working-class job. Witness, for example, the TV sports commercials for beer or trucks: the men laughing together in Levis, getting off work at the factory or the oil rig, gathering around the frosty beer keg or striking out cross-country with four-wheel drive. Male fellowship seems to belong to working-class men. In commercials, the middle-class businessman in his three-piece suit is most often pictured alone, perhaps sprinting toward his rent-a-car; if he is with another person, it often is a woman who's sharing a romantic scene in a commercial for wine—unlike those for beer.

Our culture urges men to achieve, to reach a higher socio-economic status, and then it equates such achievement with losing male fellowship, even scorning it as lower class.

At the same time, none of us really wants to work as hard as our forefathers did; indeed, it's unlikely any of them wanted their sons to toil so. Yet today, we judge ourselves by their standard. We struggle with an inner sense that we should not have to suffer at our jobs as our fathers and grandfathers did. Yet, if we do not, we are not as masculine as they were.

A man's struggle for masculine identity through work is therefore linked with his struggle to bond with the father, with the men from whom he comes. That's why educated sons of working-class fathers may find themselves unable to affirm their white-collar professions as "manly" if their jobs separate them from their fathers' work. We may feel obliged to push ourselves to the point of physical exhaustion at our offices in an effort to measure up to the "manly" physical/muscular standard of our fathers' jobs.

This inner struggle was portrayed graphically in Alan, unemployed at age thirty-five and frustrated by his lifelong inability to decide what kind of job he really wanted. He had quit his last job as a printing press operator, and hoped now to work as a musician.

Exploring his childhood, I discovered that Alan's father had been a carpenter who spent many hours in his basement workshop designing and building. The mother, however, was determined that her son would have a "better" job than his father. During his childhood, she pushed Alan into dramatics, music lessons, and extracurricular cultural programs. In school, he had won many awards for his acting and musical ability. He "just naturally" went to college, but became depressed in his junior year when he could not decide upon a major field of study, and dropped out. Next he joined an Eastern cult; after several years, he left and converted to Christianity. As devoted to his church and prayer life as he had been to the cult, he still remained lost and confused in his life goals.

Clearly, Alan had drawn impetus for his professional future from his mother, and his ultimate confusion over the right job suggested an inadequate bonding with the father. When we had become comfortable talking together, I focused accordingly.

"What are your most vivid memories of your father?" I asked at one point.

Knitting his brow, Alan sighed. "I guess we really never talked that much together," he said, then fell silent.

"Whether or not you talked much with your father, what do you remember most clearly about him?" I continued, hoping to reveal at least one memory-clue in his sense of being cut off from masculine strength and determination. Quietly, I prayed and asked the Holy Spirit to bring to Alan's mind a memory that might lead to such an inner wound, and so to a significant healing.

After several moments, he sighed again.

"I remember one late afternoon, coming home from after-school drama practice. I still had to do my piano lesson. I was walking through the kitchen, on my way to the den where the piano was. The basement door was in the kitchen, and that day it was open. As I passed by, I could hear my father downstairs sawing and then pounding some nails." He hesitated. "I just kind of stopped there by the open door and looked down into the basement. It was dark, but a bright light was on over to the side where my father was. I couldn't see him, but I could hear him working."

He stopped talking, and I waited. Finally, I spoke: "And what did you do?"

"I guess I just stood there for a minute . . . and then I remembered my piano lesson, and I turned and went into the den."

"What did it feel like, standing there at the top of the basement stairs?" I asked.

"A little scary," he said at once, then added, ". . . but kind of good, too."

"Did you want to go down into the basement with your father?"

"I couldn't. I had to get to my piano lesson."

Gently, I pushed on: "But did you want to?"

Silence. And then: "I . . . I don't know."

I decided it was time to raise the sword. "Do you want to go down into the basement with your father—now?"

"Wh-what do you mean?"

"I mean, that I see your whole life as basically standing in the kitchen, at the top of the basement stairs, literally between your mother and your father, between the basement workshop's deep, physical, manly call, and the piano's artistic, mental, feminine call. I see you trapped by your fear, unable to move wholeheartedly in either direction, as fearful of bonding with your father as of disobeying or disappointing your mother."

He thought for a moment. "You mean, you think that's why I keep going back and forth between jobs like working with my hands at the printing press and playing music?"

"It could well be," I replied. "In any case, I think that you may need to go down into that basement and meet your father before you can ever be comfortable with yourself as a man and know what sort of job is really right for you."

"But . . . how can I go down into that basement now?" he asked, puzzled. "I mean, that was all in the past."

"Was it?" I replied. "Your job situation right now suggests that it's awfully current."

He continued his confused look, and I proceeded. "I know Jesus can walk you down those steps and introduce you to your father as He knows him. Would you be willing to let Him do that?"

He paused a moment. "Well . . . OK; let's try it."

"Can you picture yourself as a boy standing there at the top of the basement stairs?" I asked. As he closed his eyes and nodded, I invited him to ask Jesus to stand there with him, take his hand and walk with him down to where his father was.

"OK," he said. And then, "Jesus and I are now standing by my dad. It's kind of dark in the basement, but it's bright beside Jesus and my father."

"Why don't you tell your father how you're feeling right now, and how you've felt standing up there at the kitchen doorway?"

A pause. "Well . . . OK. Dad, I . . . I've known you were down here and . . . I've felt . . . alone and apart from you. I've wanted to be close to you . . . but I guess . . . I've been afraid of disappointing Mom and getting her upset."

He stopped. I waited, then asked, "What's Jesus doing?"

"He's got one hand on Dad's shoulder and the other on my shoulder. It's funny, but it's like Dad understands—because he's been afraid of upsetting Mom, too! He's wanted to be closer to me, but he didn't think I wanted to be closer to him. He thought I'd rather be with Mom."

"Why don't you tell your dad how you've felt about him and his work?" I suggested.

"Dad, I . . . I guess I just didn't think your work was all that worthwhile. I'm sorry . . . I really wanted to be with you . . . so much . . ."

Tears formed in Alan's eyes, and I waited.

"Dad just seems to understand. And . . . oh! Now I see! His own mother was so pushy and scared him when he was a boy—just like me. So he was scared to go against my mother, too! It's true—I remember Gramma had a sharp edge lots of times—just like Mom."

He fell silent.

"Jesus is pulling Dad and me together. We're hugging each other . . . oh, Dad!" Alan sat quietly, glowing.

Later, Alan reflected on what had happened. "I'd just sort of judged Dad the way Mom did, like his tools and work were too earthy or something. But now I realize I've wanted to have a lot of the good qualities I'd rejected in him. In fact, those parts of him are really a part of me, but I'd suppressed them in me just as I rejected them in him. No wonder I've always been torn between working with my hands, like at the printing machines, and being artistic, like with music."

As Alan talked, I shared with him a sense that through that vision prayer, the Father God was calling him down to the "basement of his soul," so to speak, to look deeper into himself for the tools of life ministry the Father had given him.

A week later, Alan called and said he had called his father back East and essentially apologized for not recognizing his good qualities, and telling him at last, "I really love you, Dad." To Alan's surprise and deep joy, his father had said that when he died, he wanted Alan to have his tools.

Shortly after that Alan began working as a piano tuner, buying the necessary tools, and also as a music-recording-studio technician. I remarked that both jobs seemed the perfect melding of both the "earthy tools" of his father and the artistic music of his mother.

Often the lack of such simple communication between father and son about their genuine feelings for one another can create misunderstandings which endure and stunt a boy's later sense of usefulness and productivity. I once prayed with a man, for example, who had stayed just three years in his first job after graduate school, then left and floated to a variety of jobs, from realtor to musician. At the age of thirty-seven, he had recently been divorced by his Ph.D. wife. I was not then alert to the need for father-son bonding, and after we had chatted awhile I had no idea how to help him. Finally, I suggested we pray, and he agreed.

Almost as soon as we bowed our heads, an image came to my mind of a young man in a suit; behind him and off to one side, as if in the shadows, stood an older man in rough overalls. As I offered a "standard" prayer for God to help us, the image remained; after a few moments of silence, I decided to share it with David. "Does that picture mean anything to you?" I asked matter-of-factly.

To my surprise, David's head dropped into his hands and he began to cry. For perhaps ten minutes I sat quietly waiting as he sobbed. Then he explained.

"I was raised on a farm in the Midwest," he began. "I was the only high school graduate in the family. I worked hard at my studies—even though I felt guilty for not being able to be out in the field working with Dad all the time." When graduation day approached, David had spent some of his allowance and savings for a suit.

"I wanted my father to be so proud of me," he declared, his eyes filling with tears again. "Then all he did was drive me to the graduation ceremony in our pickup, and let me off. He never stayed to see me graduate. He just came and picked me up afterward."

Clearly, this memory of the father's emotional abandonment had deeply wounded David years earlier, on the threshold of manhood. I asked if he could remember riding home from the graduation ceremony with his father in the truck. He nodded, and I then suggested that we pray again—this time, bringing that memory back to mind, and asking Jesus to be with him there in the cab with his father.

David bowed his head, and asked Jesus to be with him and his father in that farm truck almost twenty years earlier.

For several minutes I prayed quietly, then asked, "What's happening?"

"Jesus put His arm around my Dad and me. I told my Dad how much it hurt me that he didn't stay and see me graduate, how hard I'd worked at school to make him proud of me like that." David sighed. "And you know what? Dad said he'd really wanted to be there, but he felt so embarrassed and out of place at an academic function like that, his being an uneducated farmer and all, like he just wasn't good enough."

"Now that you understand your Dad wasn't really rejecting you, but just operating out of his own fear of rejection, do you think you can forgive him?" I said.

David smiled, and nodded. "I forgive you, Dad!" he said. "And I thank you for all the hard work you put in to provide for the family. You're a super dad, and I love you!" Tears came again to David's eyes—this time for joy.

As members of the transitional generation, both Alan and David portray graphically the struggle among men today for manly direction in their work. Even second-generation educated men, however, participate in this struggle between their working-class grandfathers and their white-collar fathers. My own story of the boots is a clear example.

My father is a retired Naval officer with an M.B.A. degree. His father, however, had been forced to leave third grade to work in the factories near Philadelphia. After standing sixty hours a week, year after year, beside a blazing steel-mill furnace, he died of cancer at age fifty-four—with virtually no pension to show for his work. My father recalls the thick wool shirts his father wore as protection from the red-hot sparks; after work, his mother would peel the sweat-soaked shirt off my grandfather's back very slowly, so as not to irritate the many burn wounds that pockmarked his body.

At the age of forty-two, I visited my father's hometown for the first time—not that I hadn't wanted to earlier. This town had always called to my heart, if not my very soul, for I had heard my father tell of its boyhood charms many times.

A year earlier, I had left my full-time local church pastorate to set out on my own "freelance ministry" of writing and teaching. That year had not been very productive. I had finished one book manuscript, which had been rejected by over twenty publishers; I had secured no more than half a dozen teaching evenings at various churches. Amid clouds of self-doubt, I procrastinated, and punished myself. Was I a fool to have left the security of the parish? Did I really have anything that important to offer? Was I just not good enough to hold down a "real job"?

During this time, I received a letter from the twenty-year-old grandson of my father's sister; he had begun researching the family tree and was inviting me to come back East and let him give me a tour of my Dalbey roots. At first, I declined graciously. But then, I saw a denominational conference being held just a few miles away from that area. Could I afford to take the time and go? After all, I had been so inefficient in my work. . . .

I could not know at the time that visiting my father's hometown would provide precisely the focus I needed to motivate me in my work and to help me recognize the "real job" to which God had called me.

In the end, I decided that the church conference justified the trip, and I went—though not without a guilty conscience.

After the conference, my cousin Jeff, whom I had never met, picked me up and took me to visit my aunt, his eighty-nine-year-old grandmother. I had seen her only once, perhaps thirty-five years earlier. As we greeted each other and chatted, I studied her face and yes, the resemblance was there: my father's blue eyes, broad chin, high forehead! Later that evening, as I brushed my teeth before going to bed, I hesitated before the bathroom mirror. Cautiously, I set my toothbrush aside and leaned closer. Yes, it was there! The eyes, the chin, the forehead . . . my father was there! And then it struck me: who was there in my father, in his sister, in all of us?

The next day, I stood before the very millworkers' house where my father's parents had lived after their wedding in 1900. Little more than a carlength wide, joined on either side by other "houses" in the row, and dotted with two tiny windows, my grandfather's house gazed at me. *What in the world must it be like in there during the hot, humid summers?* Below me lay a brick sidewalk, worn smooth and uneven by years of wear. My grandfather had stepped on these very bricks on his way to the steel mill each morning, coming home each night in his sweat-soaked wool shirt.

Later, I walked up the stairs, now covered with weeds, to the ugly, sooty-brick buildings where my grandfather had worked. Guarded by tall, silent smokestacks and laced with broken windows, the deserted steel mill rested in strange peace, a skeleton whose workers had long passed away. Standing there, I imagined my grandfather sitting as my grandmother peeled off his wool shirt. Involuntarily, I winced.

And then, I wept. Tears poured out of me. Tears of the

father, the son, the grandson . . . tears of anger, of repentance, of loss . . . I wept.

Hours afterward, I stood before the tire and rubber factory where my father had worked after high school, breathing its foul air and suffering its heavy loads until he stood up one day and declared, "There must be something more to life than this." And I stood on the platform of the train station—now an antique shop—where my father stood after work at the factory, waiting for the train that took him to college in the city. On that train he met the person who introduced him to my mother.

The next day, we went to the churchyard where my father's grandfather and great-grandfather are buried. Sitting there on a grassy knoll overlooking the lush countryside, I touched my great-great grandfather Edmund Dalbey's name—now barely visible on the simple flat white tombstone.

I tried to imagine a team of horses pulling a wagon up to the spot, and men lifting Edmund's casket out. Was it a sunny day like today? Or cold and rainy? What did the pastor say about Edmund and his life? I wondered: what had Edmund wanted for his son? Indeed, what had his son wanted from Edmund?

After awhile, I found his son Richard's grave, marked by a large, polished granite stone and including his wife's name, MARGARET GRIFFITH. Clearly, Richard's children had been able to provide more for their father than Richard had for his.

Richard, I knew, had been a marine in the Union navy during the Civil War. I discovered this when my aunt showed me five letters Richard had written to his mother when he served aboard the *U.S.S. Sabine* which had been sent to intercept Confederate gun runners during the war. His handwriting was awkward and his spelling largely phonetic; still, one particularly revealing section leapt out at me. Apparently, like any lonely sailor far from home, he had written his mother earlier and asked her to send him a box of needed items:

> i am sory that i sent for a box for i am afraid that you cant spare the money fore to send it i am to owt don [too outdone] that you have gone to work in the mill fore i am afrade that you will cripple

youre selfe dragen up and down that hill this winter you didnt say
what mill you were working in nor what you were doing there you
sade some time agoe that you coldent see how to so [sew] or reede
eny more without spects and you coldnt help so i cant make out
what yowe are a doing un less yourure a spooling and wages must
have been razied or less yow codent get three dolars a weak not at
old farleys fore that all that he pays old hands. . . .

Clearly, the women in my heritage had worked hard, too,
even winding wool thread onto spools for three dollars a week.

That same afternoon, I hiked up the hill to where the old
Dalbey home had been. Panting at the top, I realized why Richard
had been so concerned for his mother's safety during the winter
months! Later, my aunt told me that her father had carried her
piggyback up that hill many times to visit her grandmother Dalbey.

To my great disappointment, the houses beyond the hill-
top—including my great-great grandfather's—had been razed for
the freeway below. Many other homes remained along the steep
street, however, and as I walked down I saw an old man outside
with a shovel, digging a ditch to lay pipe. I greeted him, and told
him that my ancestors had lived on that very street. "I'm Gordon
Dalbey," I said, extending my hand. "Maybe you've heard my
name before?"

Setting his shovel aside, he wiped his hand on his trousers
and reached out to shake my hand. "I'm Frank Griffith," he said.

"GRIFFITH?" I exclaimed before he could say another word.
"My great-grandmother was a Griffith!"

As I boarded my return flight to California later that week, I
knew I would never be the same. I had come to that place a world
traveler, rootless, unfocused, even careless with my life, as if I had
been cast out into the world from no real place and with no real
identity or lasting purpose.

I returned a son—a man who comes from a place, from
specific men, and who is responsible to make the most of his own
role in history as they did in theirs.

Several weeks after I returned, friends began to remark that
I seemed somehow "stronger," "more willing to speak up," more

"focused." I set out a five-day writing schedule that included six hours a day at the typewriter and at least three days with exercise: weightlifting, jogging, tennis. I soon began to realize how I had allowed certain others to take advantage of me, and I decided to stand up for myself; some of these others left me, others began to treat me with more respect. Within six months I had finished my second book manuscript, *The Making of a Spiritual Warrior*.

I know at last that I am a working man. I may never need cowboy boots to do my job—the job to which God has called me. I do not work out of guilt, but I recognize now my responsibility to do what I can with the gifts God has given me to make this world a better place. To do any less would profane the Dalbey men who went before me, whose suffering made my life today easier.

At the age of thirty-three, my grandfather looked ahead at twenty more years of sweating beside a steel-mill furnace. At the same age, I held master's degrees from Stanford and Harvard, and began my ministry. The only callouses on my hand were from playing tennis. What in the world, I have often wondered, would I say to my grandfather if he were alive today? The same thing I say to my father himself: "Thank you."

To God, I say, "Forgive me. I am too comfortable, too lazy. I worry about trifles, and I take so much for granted. Save me, Lord, from the presumption that I have earned what I have by my own efforts, alone, that I am 'my own man.' Help me, Lord, to be faithful to the sacrifices of the men who came before me, on whose shoulders I stand today—and out of that, to be faithful to your sacrifice for me in Jesus."

To myself, I say, "Remember and never forget where you come from." And I read again and again that commandment to my forebears in faith:

> When you come into the land which the Lord your God gives you as an inheritance, and have taken possession of it and live in it, you shall take some of the first of all the fruit of the ground, which you harvest from your land that the Lord your God gives you, and you shall put it in a basket, and you shall go to the place

which the Lord your God will choose, to make his name to dwell there. And you shall go to the priest who is in office at that time, and say to him, "I declare this day to the Lord your God that I have come into the land which the Lord swore to our fathers to give us." Then the priest shall take the basket from your hand, and set it down before the altar of the Lord your God.

And you shall make response before the Lord your God, "A wandering Aramean was my father . . . " (Deut. 26:1-5 RSV).

10
The
Father and
the Man:
Of Sons and Daughters

> But before the great and terrible day of the Lord comes, I will send
> you the prophet Elijah. He will bring fathers and children together
> again; otherwise, I would have to come and destroy your country
> (Mal. 4:5, 6).

AS THE FINAL TWO VERSES of the Hebrew canon proclaim, God's
ultimate saving action in this world is based upon a reconciliation
between fathers and their children. This presumes that fathers
have been apart from their sons and daughters, and so have lost
the essential bonding between generations which allows God to
exercise His saving power among us.

Because every earthly father is an imperfect human being, he
can never meet the profound need we all have for fatherly love.
The question for fathers, therefore, is not *whether* they will hurt
their children, but will they be willing to recognize it *when* they do

and then seek reconciliation? At the same time, the text does not place the entire burden for such reconciliation upon the father, but allows the child to initiate it as well.

In any case, the biblical faith understands that healing between fathers and children is not simply a psychological exercise to bring greater peace of mind; instead, it is the essential prerequisite to fulfilling God's purposes on earth. When fathers are reconciled with sons and daughters, God's saving power is released among us; conversely, when fathers and children remain at odds with one another, powers of destruction are beckoned.

Significantly, it is the fathers and not the mothers upon whom God focuses His call for reconciliation in the Last Days. Perhaps this reflects God's view that mothers are likely to care more deeply about their children than fathers, since the child was for nine months literally part of the mother's body. Legal customs reflect this. Jewish lineage, for example, is based on the mother; one is a Jew only if born of a Jewish mother, because the identity of one's mother is more easily ascertained than that of one's father, who may not be present and committed to the "family." Unlike the father, the mother cannot choose to be apart from the child, whom she carries in her own body.

Even as I was typing these words, a pregnant woman called telling me about her recent visit to her doctor's office. There, she overheard two pregnant teenagers commiserating that their boyfriends had left them once their sexual pleasure led to such consequences.

Much concern for child care in both church and secular society focuses on how to get working mothers back into the home. God's ultimate concern, however, is not in bringing mothers and children together again, but, as the Hebrew canon states, in bringing "*fathers* and children together again." This clearly implies that once fathers assume their primary and godly role in the family, all other family relationships proceed properly.

Consider, for example, the pregnant teenage girls at my friend's doctor's office. If they had received godly affection and discipline from their fathers, they would not have been so vulnerable to their boyfriends' advances. If the boyfriends had received proper affection and discipline from their own fathers, they would not have been so likely to take advantage of the girl—or, if she were the initiator, to fall to her temptations.

Because the reconciliation of fathers and children is so pivotal in God's plan for earth, I offer two Bible stories that suggest helpful guidelines: one portraying a father and son, the other describing a father and daughter:

The Giant-Killer and His Son

"O Absalom, my son, my son!" (2 Sam. 18:33)

At thirty-one, Peter came to me bearing a host of self-doubts. A graduate of a prestigious private university and an accomplished professional man, he nevertheless seemed constantly to judge himself as inadequate. His pattern suggested a lack of manly affirmation from the father, and before long I inquired how his father might have shown love for him. Peter responded quickly, as if to defend his father.

"Dad never was one for giving compliments or hugging and stuff like that," he declared. "But I know he loved me."

"How do you know he loved you?" I asked matter-of-factly.

"What do you mean?"

I realized that, without having experienced any outward demonstration of fatherly love, Peter could not understand my question. "I only mean, what did your father do which led you to believe he loved you?"

Peter shifted uncomfortably. "Well, like I said, Dad wasn't much for a lot of outward display. I just kind of sensed he loved me, that's all."

Quickly, I prayed: *Lord, should I drop this issue, or pursue it further?* Sensing that the Lord had a plan in going further, I continued. "Did your father ever say to you, 'You're my son, Peter, and I love you'?"

For the first time that hour, Peter sat quietly for a moment before speaking. "No," he replied finally, a trace of wistfulness in his voice. "I can't recall him ever saying anything like that."

"It sounds as if you wish he might have said that," I noted.

At that, Peter began to talk about his genuine longing for his father's affection, and wishing his father might have "come right out and said things like that."

Over the next few weeks, we prayed often for healing in Peter through knowing the Father God's love. And then, one day, he remarked, "I wonder what Dad would say if I just came out and asked him, 'Do you love me?'"

I hesitated, then decided to explore the possibility. As we talked it over, Peter declared that in fact, he was ready to do just that, and he decided to write a letter to his father, who lived in a distant city.

Peter wrote the letter, asking the question, and we waited—not without some fear on his part. Several weeks later, he came into my office with a letter in his hand.

"Dad wrote me back," he said, a puzzled look on his face.

"What did he say?"

"He says, 'I'm glad you asked me the question, and I'm sorry you didn't know. Of course, I love all my children.'"

I found myself puzzled also. "What do you make of that?"

"Well . . . I guess that's my answer . . . I mean, that's all I'm going to get from him."

"You sound disappointed," I noted.

"Well, it took a lot of courage for me to write and ask Dad if he loves me," Peter began. "And he still didn't come right out and say 'Yes.' It's not what I'd hoped for . . . but I don't know if I'm willing to push him any further."

"What are you afraid might happen if you pushed further?" I asked.

Peter fell silent, then smiled nervously. "I'm sure you know—that he might say 'No'."

Gently, I noted that his fear indicated that contrary to his cavalier response weeks earlier, he really hadn't been sure then—or ever?—of his father's love.

I waited, then spoke. "So what are you going to do?"

Peter sighed. "I know what I've got to do sooner or later. I started this out, and I've got to ride it all the way to the end. I didn't ask Dad if he loved 'all his children,' but if he loved me. I guess I've got to just say that to him, and ask him again."

I could only affirm Peter's courage in deciding to do so.

Again we waited for a reply, dealing meanwhile with Peter's

fear of losing his father's love and the deep anger that idea prompted within him. And then, at last, the letter came.

"I can't believe it!" Peter said, smiling and shaking his head as he waved his father's letter at me. "Listen to what Dad says: 'I have to thank you for pushing me with your question. I guess I hadn't really thought that deeply about it before. But when I did think about it, I realized that I do love you, Peter, and I need to say that for myself probably as much as you may need to hear it.'"

To my surprise, I found myself sighing in relief and smiling with Peter—sensing that his story may well touch all men. Whether he is three or thirty-one the son longs to know his father loves him, and without some clear demonstration of that, the resulting uncertainty can spawn crippling self-doubts and destructive anger.

My own personal reaction to Peter's story—and similar reactions in other male friends with whom I shared it—led me to sense a universal quality in it. As I reflected on it, I realized that the essence of this story was portrayed thousands of years ago in the biblical account of King David and his son, Absalom.

The dramatic climax of that story is widely recognized in David's mourning cry, "O Absalom, my son, my son!" At first, these words seem to portray a sad, but not unusual, case in which the son has died in war. But what was sad becomes tragic when we realize that the war was *between* King David and Absalom. Father and son had been battling *each other*. They had allowed so much pain and fear and anger to build up between them that they yielded themselves to death, saying that death is king, that only death can resolve the dispute.

The tragic story begins (2 Sam. 13) with Absalom and his sister Tamar—both children by the same mother—and Amnon, David's oldest son by another wife. Amnon rapes his half-sister Tamar, and her brother Absalom naturally hates him for doing so. But since Amnon is David's oldest son, by the ancient Hebrew custom he stands as his father's heir. David is therefore bound to favor him over all his other children. So Amnon gets off virtually scot-free; though David is "furious," the Bible records no discipline meted out to Amnon.

Absalom, meanwhile, refuses to speak to his brother Amnon (13:22). He just sits, quiet and rigid, like a hungry animal watching its prey, biding his time. He is simmering with anger, the bottled-up kind that can only explode. He resents his older brother not only for what he did, but for getting away with it. The focus of Absalom's anger, in fact, has begun to shift away from Amnon to his father David, who apparently disregards Absalom's feelings.

The younger son's deep sense of frustration in the face of his father's injustice foreshadows violence. Yet, even as he bitterly resents his older brother and father, Absalom has a real choice in how he acts. No law dictates that he must explode violently, trusting death to solve the problem.

He could trust in God's reconciling love. He could go directly to his father—in the spirit in which Peter wrote to his father—and say, "Dad, you know there's no excuse for what Amnon did to my sister Tamar. But what hurts me even worse is that you just don't seem to care how I feel. You make me feel like I don't matter at all to you, and the pain from that feels like it could kill me!"

Absalom could open his heart to his father and say, "Dad, just between you and me—do you love me?" He could take that death-defying leap and say, "Dad, tell me that I'm *your* son, that you love me no matter what—even if I'm not heir to your throne, like Amnon."

What courage that would take! What boldness, what risk and daring! What faith in God's renewing, life-giving love!

Yet how much easier it is for a man to hold it all down deep inside and let it simmer; how much easier it sometimes seems to kill than to confess you need someone else's love.

But the younger son does not have the courage to be honest with himself and his father. Instead, through a series of scheming lies, Absalom has Amnon killed. Then, since he has murdered the king's heir, he flees his father for his mother's hometown.

With a broad stroke, the biblical historian paints the picture: "Absalom, having escaped to Geshur, stayed there three years; and David's heart went out to him with longing, for he became reconciled to the death of Amnon" (2 Sam. 13:38, 39 NEB).

"Reconciled" emotionally, David now has the choice: With a heart full of longing, he could call his son home, embrace him and say, "Let's put all this terrible pain behind us, Absalom. You *are* my son and I have missed you. You were wrong to kill your brother, but as I forgave him for dishonoring Tamar, so I now forgive you." David could at last say proudly and joyfully, "Absalom, my son, my son!"

Yet how much easier for a man to slay enemy warriors, to administer a great kingdom—indeed to kill a Philistine giant with a pebble—than to confess his love to his child face-to-face, as two adults!

And so, in a foolish confirmation of "like father, like son," David chose to hold it all inside. In fact, we see here why Absalom could not be honest about his own feelings earlier: because his father had not shown him how. Only because a "wise woman" tricks him into it, does David call Absalom home.

The reunion scene which follows is crucial to understanding the timeless and universal dimension of this story among fathers and sons. After chapters describing their longing for one another, after three long years of separation, we read one single verse: "He summoned Absalom, who came and prostrated himself humbly before the king; and he greeted Absalom with a kiss" (2 Sam. 14:33 NEB).

Period. That's all there is. Someone is summoned, he bows humbly before "the king," and there follows a kiss—the very casual, everyday greeting, like shaking hands, between men in the Middle East even today.

Something is notoriously absent here. Where is the father? Where is the son? What happened to all the deep longing, the pain, the tears, the joy? All we see here are people bowing and shaking hands, the same old violent reluctance, the same old tragic unwillingness of father and son to confess their deep love for one another. The true feelings, the true people, hide behind some terrible sense of "what men are supposed to do."

Not surprisingly, the very next sentence has Absalom plotting against his father, David: "After this, Absalom provided himself with a chariot and horses and an escort of fifty men" (2 Sam. 15:1 TEV).

Four years later, through his trickery, Absalom has won

enough supporters to declare himself king over David, who takes to the hills with his remaining loyalists.

The story that follows would rival Hollywood's greatest adventures—full of spies and counter-spies, messengers hiding in wells, and a nation hanging in the balance. In the end, David has the best spies, and he engineers the decisive battle. But before he sends his troops to meet Absalom's, he calls his commanders together and gives them very special orders: "'For my sake, don't harm the young man Absalom.' And all the troops heard David give this command to his officers" (2 Sam. 18:5).

By this point, we are almost surprised to hear David speaking with such care for his son, even before his men. He certainly never spoke that way to Absalom himself; why should he now?

The answer, certainly, is that David *does* care very deeply for his son. But for some terrible reason—did his own father, Jesse, never tell David as a boy?—he cannot say it to his son's face. The father can tell his commanders and colleagues how deeply he cares, but he can't tell the son himself. This is the stuff that tragedies are made of—now as then.

And sure enough, in the battle that follows, young Absalom is killed. David is crushed. Crying shamelessly in front of everyone, he stumbles to the chamber atop the city gate, collapses and cries, "O my son! Absalom, my son, my son Absalom. If only I had died instead of you! O Absalom, my son, my son."

The feelings are there! David *does* love his son, even more than his own life. Furthermore, David claims Absalom as his own: "Absalom, *my* son." That was what the son had needed so desperately to hear from his father when he was alive. Fathers and sons may ask each other, "Do you love me?" But the real question they're asking is, "Am I yours? Do you claim me as your own? Do you value me enough to affirm that I am a part of you?"

Indeed, the God of love did not bind with His chosen people by saying, "I love you," but rather, "I will be your God and you will be my people" (Lev. 26:12). God's love is a matter of belonging to each other, and God uses the model of father and son to portray His relationship with Israel: When Israel was a child, I loved him and called him out of Egypt as my son" (Hos. 11:1).

In their pain and fear, therefore, David and Absalom locked God out and gave death final power over their life together. Just as Absalom could see no answer to his pain except death, so David, even as he mourned his son atop the city gates, could see no answer to his pain except to have died in place of his son. Surely, Absalom's very name embodies the bitter irony of the story, for it combines the two most familiar Hebrew words, *abba* and *shalom*, meaning "peace of the father."

This ancient story of God's men says that something between father and son dies when the love God has given each for the other is not expressed openly. In fact, the story shows, our fear of doing so can have lethal consequences. The converse is true also: when fathers and sons directly express their love, each bears life to the other. And this heralds the coming day of the Lord, when the God of life "will bring fathers and children together again."

Fathers and Daughters: Letting Go of Daddy's Little Girl

Between father and son, the major issue seems to be one of bonding: Can the father draw close to the boy, express his love and care openly, and declare, "You are mine"? With his daughter, however, the energies seem to be reversed. The major issue between father and daughter is one of separation: Can the father let go of the girl, express his confidence in her abilities, and declare, "You are your own person"?

Fathers seem to bond more readily with their daughters than with their sons—likely because the boy, who potentially bears manly strength, is perceived as a competitive threat to the father's dominion.

The father's fear of his son's masculinity is quite real and must be faced to head off David-Absalom hostilities. I was startled once in a basketball locker room by a middle-aged man who had often praised his multi-talented teenage son to the other men there. Matter-of-factly, he mentioned to the rest of us that he had recently played one-on-one against his son. A pregnant pause followed. Then the father's face lit up. "And I beat him!" he proclaimed, smiling definitively and raising a fist as the others nodded in approval.

Not only does the daughter bear no such competitive threat, but in our homophobic culture, a father feels more comfortable expressing affection to his daughter than to his son. The terrible irony here is that so many fathers believe that for them to show affection for their sons will "make the boy a sissy" when precisely the opposite is true, as detailed in chapter 7. Instead, such an attitude suggests that the father himself is afraid of being seen as unmanly. Certainly, this is the fear that is communicated to the son by an emotionally distant father, thus making it even harder for the boy to bond with the masculine and easier to become vulnerable to homosexuality. A boy may even note his father's apparent preference for the sister, and try to be more feminine himself in order to draw the father's affection, as she does.

The father also is drawn to his daughter simply because a man seeks a woman like himself, in order to avoid conflict and insure security in a relationship. Every man longs for a woman created in his own image; and no woman so literally embodies this quality as his own daughter. The wife is defined by her decision to marry; the daughter is defined by her genetic makeup. The wife is not of the husband's flesh, but the daughter is. The wife can say, "You are no longer my husband." But the biological daughter can never say, "You are no longer my father." Marriage is fragile, lasting only as long as the partners agree; daughterhood lasts forever.

Apart from the growing incidence of father-daughter molestation, many fathers commit emotional incest with their daughters. "Your mother just wouldn't understand," many women report their fathers' having told them when initiating intimate conversation.

The father's reluctance to let go of his daughter has framed the sub-plot in several popular films of the last decade. *Coal Miner's Daughter*, a biography of country singer Loretta Lynn, acknowledges by its very title the father's decisive role in his daughter's life. But the model portrayed is basically negative, in which the father clings desperately to his daughter—and her feelings for him often draw her back from a life of her own. "You're my shinin' bride," he protests when she is about to become another man's wife.

Similarly, the story of *Norma Rae* portrays a woman who spearheads the first labor organization among southern textile workers. She succeeds only by overcoming her authoritarian father, who storms about demanding that she account to him for her time and activities, even when she is widowed with a child.

On Golden Pond added a compelling dimension to the issue because stars Henry and Jane Fonda were real-life father and daughter. Often during promotional interviews, Jane spoke of her girlhood longing for her father's approval, leading into years of struggling with anorexia-bulimia. In the movie itself, the adult daughter struggles against her father's self-centered, critical attitude. "Why do I always feel like a fat, ugly little girl around him?" she cries out at one point. Later, she appears in a bikini at the lake—clearly slim and attractive—and dives off a board before her diving-coach father. His restrained nod and smile at her diving form hints at the daughter's lifetime of pain and longing, performing for the father's approval.

In pop music, the father-daughter bond was caricatured during the fifties by Peggy Lee's hit song, "My Heart Belongs to Daddy." Perhaps more than any other example, such a song reflects the profound difference between the dynamic of father-daughter and that of mother-son; imagine, for example, Frank Sinatra's crooning "My Heart Belongs to Mommy."

Father-son songs, on the other hand, usually describe the separation of the two and a longing for the bond that has never been experienced. Barry Manilow's "Ships in the Night," portrays a son's longing for closeness with his father, as they pass through life without ever touching each other at any significant level. In Johnny Cash's "A Boy Named Sue," the father has named his son "Sue" precisely because he would not be with the boy to rear him. When years later a grownup Sue meets his father at last, the two battle furiously—shades of Absalom and David—but finally embrace. Surely, every cheering inmate at Folsom Prison, where

Cash first recorded that song, understood all too well this implicit longing of son for father and its concomitant anger. And so does the average man today understand it, insofar as he is imprisoned, himself, by the same unfulfilled longing and unresolved anger.

Clearly, the difficulty in properly fathering a daughter is in how to demonstrate enough love and affirmation for her to know she is lovable and capable, without preventing her from experiencing that love and achievement among others, as she must in order to grow.

I do not believe that any human father can accomplish this with his own will power and wisdom. I believe the father's bond with his daughter is intrinsic to the self-centered nature of human flesh. And somehow, the father must come to face squarely this self-centered root of his relationship with his daughter, and take it to the Cross. He must confess there his own inability to be the father God wants him to be for his daughter. In so doing, the man allows the Father God to give him His Holy Spirit to guide him in fatherhood, so that he lets his daughter go, not to the world, but to the true Father God—that she might at last discover her true self as His daughter.

A surprisingly clear model for a father's brutal self-honesty and yielding his daughter to God is portrayed in a biblical account of Jesus' ministry.

A man named Jairus approached Jesus in great distress. Jairus was clearly a well-known religious figure, for the text identifies him as "an official in the local synagogue":

> He threw himself down at Jesus' feet and begged him to go to his home, because his only daughter, who was twelve years old, was dying (Luke 8:41, 42).

We see here the distinguished leader of the religious community on his knees in the dirt, begging aloud in behalf of his beloved daughter. Surely, this shameless public display of a father's concern for his daughter was shocking in a time when fathers were publicly proud only of sons. As the psalmist declared, "The sons a man has when he is young are like arrows in a soldier's hand. Happy is the man who has many such arrows" (Ps. 127:4, 5). You might bend to help your son—your power, your arrows, your insurance—but your daughter? Well, that's women's business!

Jairus' humbling act therefore demonstrated a profound love for his daughter, a devotion deeper even than his pride before other men. And certainly, any cowboy can tell you that nothing in this world matters more than riding tall in the saddle before other men.

Yet even as he loved his daughter, in going to Jesus for help, Jairus accepted his own limitations and relinquished his image of independence and self-reliance—so often considered essential to a man's self-esteem. In publicly confessing his inability to provide what his daughter needed, to heal her himself, Jairus knew that he was not God.

The pain of such self-acceptance and letting go of the daughter is portrayed by Lutheran pastor Robert Herhold, who in his book, *The Promise beyond the Pain* describes this crisis of middle-aged fathers:

> The fact that a man's paid vacation has reached a plateau increases the pain of ending his career as a father. . . . The dream of becoming president of the firm . . . has vanished. Then he discovers he can still be "president" in his daughter's eyes. As he tightens his grip on that role, an inner voice tells him that he cannot have that job either. In his pain, he struggles to hold on to his child. "She still needs me a little longer. I understand her better than her friends, who are as confused as she is. I will let go as soon as she can stand on her own two feet. My role is just to support her a little longer. . . ." Then a painful voice from within whispers, "Yes, but quit while you're ahead."[1]

Significantly, Jairus' daughter was twelve years old, on the threshold of womanhood. At that point in her life, she needed a father to usher her into the world by providing a positive male image. In spiritual terms, however, she was as vulnerable to the temptation to idolize her father as he was to play God for her. But God allowed the powers of the world to intervene.

Throughout her girlhood, the daughter had likely believed that no danger could befall her so long as Daddy was near. But the onset of a fatal illness forced her—and her father—to face the fact that Daddy was not God, that he could not save her from every evil and danger in the world. Daddy, in fact, was human and thus, sometimes helpless.

While this may be a painful blow to a father's ego, it is a terrifying threat to a child's life. Here, of course, lies the turning point in faith, beyond which a daughter can become a woman as Daddy becomes a person.

An excellent road map for this passage from girlhood to adulthood through the father's letting go is Madeleine L'Engle's prizewinning book *A Wrinkle in Time.* Twelve-year-old Meg Murry is the daughter of world-famous scientists. When her father disappears, she and her little brother Charles are transported to the lair where a deadly Evil Power holds him prisoner behind a glass wall. Meg is transported through the wall, but realizes she and her father must go out again to rescue Charles:

> "Put your arms around my neck, Meg," Mr. Murry said. "Hold onto me tightly. Close your eyes and don't be afraid." For a moment, it seemed that the chill darkness would tear her from her father's arms. . . . Her father's arms tightened around her and she clung to his neck with a strangle-hold, but she was no longer lost in panic. She knew that if her father could not get her through the wall, he would stay with her rather than leave her; she knew that she was safe as long as she was in his arms.[2]

When Meg and her father are free, they find the Evil Power is about to swallow them all. "Do something!" Meg implores her father. "Do something! Help! Save us!" But all Mr. Murry can do is whisk Meg and himself away, leaving Charles and hoping to rescue the boy later.

Meg is clearly not used to seeing her father's weaknesses. Angrily, she shouts at him, "You're supposed to help! You'd better take me back to get Charles right away!"

The ugly words tumbled from her lips even as she herself could not believe that it was to her father, her beloved, longed-for father that she was talking this way. . . . She had found her father, and he had not made everything all right. Everything kept getting worse and worse. If the long search for her father was ended, and he wasn't able to overcome all their difficulties, there was nothing to guarantee that it would all come out right in the end. There was nothing left to hope for.[3]

In a word, the Daddy-god idol had fallen. Here lies death for idol-worshipping girls—or the beginning of new life for faithful women and their fathers. For indeed, only when idols fall can God arise in our lives. As Jesus noted, "Whoever loves father or mother more than me is not fit to be my disciple" (Matt. 10:37).

In the midst of this shattering realization, when all the daughter's childish hopes are lost, it becomes clear that only one person is capable of wrenching little Charles away from the Evil Power. That person is Meg, herself—because the Evil Power only can be overcome through knowing and loving, and Meg has come to know and love Charles better than anyone else in their father's absence.

The father's job at this point becomes to encourage, to let go, to hold faith in the larger Power of good.

Facing alone this dangerous mission—the task she had thought only Daddy could handle—Meg at last turns to her father:

"I'm—I'm sorry, Father." He took her hand in his, bent down to her. . . . "Sorry for what, Megatron?" Tears almost came to her eyes at the gentle use of her name. "I wanted you to do it all for me. I wanted everything to be all easy and simple . . . so I tried to pretend that it was all your fault . . . because I was scared and didn't want to have to do anything myself—"

"But I wanted to do it for you," Mr. Murry said. "That's what every parent wants." . . . . Mr. Murry sighed. He drew Meg close to him. "Little Megaparsec. Don't be afraid to be afraid. We will try to have courage for you. That is all we can do."[4]

Like the biblical account of Jairus, this story says that the finest thing a father can do for his daughter is not to promise her protection forever, but to overcome his own ego and introduce her to a Power larger than himself. This Power is love and healing and newness of life, which alone can overcome darkness and evil. It calls all fathers to become persons and all little girls to become women, as it calls all of us to become children of the Living God.

The father, therefore, must become humble enough before the Father God that he knows himself as a son of God. And this bold humility on the father's part is what frees his children to become sons and daughters of the Father God, themselves.

And this bringing "fathers and children together again" is what beckons "the great and terrible day of the Lord," in which the Father God's saving power is revealed in its fullness.

11
To
Know
the
Father

A father to the fatherless . . . is God in his holy dwelling (Ps. 68:5 NIV).

A FRIEND OF MINE who has spent his adult life in Los Angeles took his four-year-old son back to Nebraska to visit the family farm, and was startled by the boy's response there. When they walked into the barn, my friend decided to demonstrate how to milk a cow. The boy stood wide-eyed as his father grasped the udder, squirted out a cup of milk and held it up to him. To my friend's surprise, the boy drew back in disgust.

"I don't want that!" he exclaimed. "That's not real milk."

"What do you mean?" my friend asked, puzzled.

"Real milk comes from a store!" his son replied

I submit this not simply as an amusing tale of childlike innocence, but as an ominous parable of our time. For we live in a world in which human pride has unleashed a widespread deception, leading us to believe that we humans are the source of all things. Like the little boy who cannot imagine that milk comes from a cow instead of a supermarket, we in our technological age are tempted to forget life's Original Source and its power to meet our needs.

Advertising often capitalizes on this deception. Consider, for example, the beer commercials during football broadcasts. Always the action takes place in a scene projecting masculine fellowship: the bar, the oil rig, the fishing boat. Crowds of husky men laugh loudly and slap each other playfully on the back. The message is clear to a culture in which men are painfully isolated from one another: our beer instantly bestows acceptable male fellowship, and saves you from the fearful task of pursuing male friendships. Real male fellowship, the ads imply, comes from a beer bottle; the beer draws men together and overcomes alienation and rejection. Small wonder, therefore, that alcoholic men also suffer from their fathers' emotional abandonment.

Nowhere are the effects of this deception more damaging than in our attempts to meet the deepest human need: to be loved.

One couple sought my counsel amid great turmoil in their marriage. "All I ever wanted out of marriage was to be loved," the wife declared, reaching for her handkerchief. "But I never seem to get it from him!" Her husband drew back in surprise. "What do you mean, *you* don't get love from me?" he exclaimed angrily. "You never give me the love I need from you!"

I often hear husbands and wives complain that their spouse "doesn't give me enough love." Many marriages, indeed, seem mired in an angry standoff in which each partner feels unloved by the other. The biblical faith, meanwhile, is quite clear about the source of love and what it means for us humans who give and receive love. "Dear Friends," as John says in his first letter to the early church, "let us love one another, because love comes from God" (4:7).

This simple, direct statement about the ultimate source of love shatters the very foundations on which, tragically, the vast majority of our most significant human relationships are based. It declares that love—which we hunger for in the depths of our souls, which we long for in our relationships with one another, and which fills our lives with purpose—"comes from God." Note that John does not say, "Dear Friends, love one another because love comes from human beings," that is, "If you don't get love from another person, you can't be loved." Rather, John says you must first understand that love does not come from another person, but only *through* him or her *from* God.

The best that can be said about our human efforts to love one another is that we mediate God's love. That is, when we say we love another person, we are essentially receiving love from God and channeling it to him or her.

One major implication of this statement is clear: if you want to give more love to another person, you must first go to the Source and get more of it to give. If love came from human beings, then to love more would simply mean gritting your teeth and trying harder. But anyone who has attempted that path knows it leads more often to frustration at one's own inadequacy and resentment of the other's needs. Instead, Christians increase their capacity to love by confessing their own inadequacy and drawing closer to God to receive more of His love. Still, most of us go to God for love with thimbles, while He wants us to come with barrels, because as we seek the healing that would allow us to receive more of God's love, our "capacity" for giving love to others increases.

Of course, there is nothing inherently wrong with receiving love from another human being, any more than with getting your milk at the store instead of the farm. A dairy farmer might interject here that the pasteurized store milk has been stripped of many natural vitamins and minerals. And indeed, we human beings are by definition imperfect channels for God's love; by the time God's love has passed through our human nature in all its pride and selfishness, it does not often reach the other person in its original, pure form. In this present age, at best "what we see now is like a dim image in a mirror" (1 Cor. 13:12). Most of us know the experience of feeling deep love for someone—and moments later be fighting with him or her.

The danger in loving relationships is not in receiving love from another human being, but in believing that the other person is the source of that love. All of us know we need love, and if we believe it is available only from another person, our love relationships eventually take on overtones of desperation and resentment.

Granted, everything goes smoothly as long as you go to the other person for love when he or she has it to give. But in your human imperfection, eventually you will ask for love when the other has none to give. "I need to be alone now," you may hear, or even, "Go away and don't bother me!" What then?

In your heart, you reason: I must have love in order to live and grow. Only you can give it to me. Therefore, you *must* give it to me, or I shall die.

All too often, we then proceed to throttle the one we love, demanding, "Why don't you give me the love I need?!"

To do so is like pounding on the faucet when the neighborhood water main has broken: not only do you not get water, but you harm the faucet, making it less likely to deliver a full stream when the water is available again. Similarly, our demands upon the other person bring not the love we need but further resistance.

As long as we believe that love comes from the other person, we are left with two options:

First, we can give up altogether on receiving love, withdraw into a corner, build walls, and tune out on life. Who knows how many emotional disorders follow this pattern?

More likely, however, we drop back and begin scheming to manipulate the other person into giving us the love we need: we strive to perform better, we threaten, we beg, we retaliate.

The basic falsehood that fuels this upset is our conviction that the other person *can* give us the love we need. Persons I pray for often come to realize that they never received the love they needed from a particular parent. One man surfaced an intense anger toward his father. "All my life I've wanted my father to give me love," he declared, clenching his fists as the tears welled up in his eyes.

"Why do you think he didn't give it to you?" I asked.

"Well, he would rather be off at work than with me!"

"No," I said gently, but firmly, then urged him to think more deeply.

"Then it was because he's a judgmental, hard-nosed, unfeeling person!" he declared.

Again I said no, and encouraged him to examine his father's own upbringing, continuing to ask, "Why didn't he give you the love you needed?" After perhaps a half-hour of exhausting every apparent answer, the man finally slumped down in his chair and hung his head in silence. "I . . . I guess he just wasn't able to," he sighed.

I praised God, because I knew that the man had at last let go of his child's faith in Daddy and was at last on the threshold of an adult faith in God. For as long as he believed that love came from his father, he could only fear his father for wielding such power over him. But as he gave up on receiving love from his father and turned instead to God, he was set free to see his father with God's eyes—that is, to see him with compassion, as a fellow man broken by his own wounds.

Do we dare to believe that God can really give us love apart from a human mediator? We can never find out as long as we desperately cling to one another for the love which in fact no human possesses. All too often, we are led to discover the love of God only when our human partner in love is taken from us, as in divorce or death. One wonders if, indeed, God wants so badly for us to have the real thing that He might even harden the other's heart precisely when we need love most, in hopes that we will, in desperation, turn to Him at last.

The Jewish author Chaim Potok suggests such a theme in his book, *The Chosen,* which focuses on an orthodox rabbi father and his brilliant son. The latter is so gifted, and takes so much for granted, that the father decides to withhold himself and his approval from the boy in order to provide the crucible of pain and suffering in which he might learn to care for others.[1]

To discover that love comes from God we must begin by facing that embarrassingly broken part in us all that does not feel loved, no matter how sincere our loved ones may be. This is a bold step of faith, because it requires one to believe that love is still available from God directly, even without another human channel.

My experience praying with a large number of men has convinced me that the average man today remains trapped in his boyhood fear of abandonment, still believing in his broken heart that real manhood comes *from*, rather than *through* the earthly father. So he fears other men because they, too, seem to hold that awesome power over him, as his father did.

Throughout this terrible exercise in self-deception and spiritual blindness, the Father God must surely watch in agony, crying out to His beloved sons, "If only you would turn and come to me! I am love, I am what you are seeking. Sometimes you will receive a portion of my love through your father, mother, spouse, friends—but you will never receive it all through them. If you could, you would never let go of them and turn to me."

For indeed, this is the God of our ancient faith, who struggles to hold out love for us even as we turn away.

Does the man need a Father to pick him up and hold him affectionately? Listen:

I was the one who taught Israel to walk. I took my people up in my arms, but they did not acknowledge that I took care of them. I drew them to me with affection and love. I picked them up and held them to my cheek; I bent down to them and fed them. . . . How can I give you up, Israel? . . . . My heart will not let me do it! My love for you is too strong. I will not punish you in my anger. . . . For I am God and not man. I, the Holy One, am with you (Hosea 11:3–9).

Does the man need a Father who can give him strength and protect him? Listen:

The Lord says, "I am the one who strengthens you. Why should you fear mortal man, who is no more enduring than grass? Have you forgotten the Lord who made you, who stretched out the heavens and laid the earth's foundations? (Isa. 51:12, 13).

Does the man need a Father who can call him out of fearful bondage where he has little power? Listen:

> When Israel was a child, I loved him and called him out of Egypt as my son (Hosea 11:1).

Does the man need a Father who can guide him with wisdom through life? Listen:

> The path you walk may be dark indeed, but trust in the Lord, rely on your God (Isa. 50:10b).

And again,

> The Lord is compassionate, and when you cry to Him for help, He will answer you. The Lord will make you go through hard times, but He Himself will be there to teach you, and you will not have to search for Him any more. If you wander off the road to the right or the left, you will hear His voice behind you saying, "Here is the road. Follow it" (Isa. 30:19–21).

Clearly, the Scriptures describe God as having all the characteristics of the father needed by the son. At various times, some of these may come to him through his earthly father. But when they do not, he need not despair; he need only go to his heavenly Father.

In praying with men, I have seen God minister His Father-love in a variety of ways. Sometimes, a man received no love at all from his earthly father, who perhaps abandoned the mother at his birth or died early. I have simply laid hands on that man and prayed for the love of the Father to be poured out upon him, inviting the man himself to ask for the Father's love, too, as a gesture of opening his heart to receive it. Often in such cases, the man may say, "I feel warm all over," or "a peace kind of came over me." Again, he may receive a vision of himself as a little boy climbing onto Jesus' lap and being held.

I sometimes encourage a man to write down a list of things he wishes his earthly father had given him, and then offer that list to the Father God. One man's father had played semipro baseball, but never had taught his son to play; as a boy, the man had felt as if his father were judging him as inadequate or "a klutz," so he

later stayed away from sports even though he longed to participate. "Do you think the Father God can teach me how to play
baseball?" he asked, not without skepticism. Stepping out in faith,
I assured him that God could do that and urged him to pray
accordingly. I confess a fear and doubt in my heart at the time.
Yet, within a week, this man went to a Christian men's gathering
and struck up a conversation with another man; as they chatted,
both sensed a budding friendship. And then, as they were parting
and exchanging business cards, the other man mentioned that
he played softball in a local church league—in fact he had once
coached baseball—and asked if the man might want to play on
the softball team?

Another man's life was a litany of troubles with women, and
he declared, "My dad never taught me a thing about women. Do
you think the Father God can teach me about women?" I assured
him that God could show him exactly what he needed to know
about women in order to bring his relationships with them into
harmony with God's plan. When we prayed, he asked the Father
God simply, "Please teach me about women like my father never
did." I prayed quietly in the Spirit, and moments later he reported
a clear "sense" of several ways he could change his responses to
women. "I guess I've been pretty rational and cut-and-dried about
things, and women see things more in terms of relationships and
feelings," he said. "Maybe I can begin to listen a little better to my
girlfriend's feelings instead of always trying to solve every problem outright by analyzing it."

Several men have said that their fathers never called them
out to be with other men, and when we asked the Father God to
fill that void, He replied in different ways according to each man's
deeper need. One man received phone calls from two other men
shortly afterward; another man began to think of men he could
call, and did so, thanking God.

To reach such a point of crying out for the Father God's
help, a man must have been sufficiently disappointed in other
persons. Many men are trapped in such a limbo of disappointment, however, and do not realize that the way out is not to give
up all hope and withdraw, but rather, to confess their misplaced

hope in other human beings and begin to place it instead in the Father God.

When a man realizes he has gone to other persons for something only God can give, he may want very much to release his spouse, children, parents, and all others from the terrible burden of giving him complete love. He may want at last to go to the Source. But, having lived so long in the world, he very likely does not know how.

We men have been shopping for milk so long at the store that we have forgotten the way back to the farm. That is, we are so accustomed to seeking love from other persons that we do not know how to approach the Father God for it.

Christians know that the original mediator of God's love to this world is none other than Jesus Christ, who "is able, now and always, to save those who come to God through him, because he lives forever to plead with God for them" (Heb. 7:25).

Thus Jesus declared to his followers,

> "I am the way, the truth, and the life; no one goes to the Father except by me. Now that you have known me," he said to them, "you will know my Father also, and from now on you do know him and you have seen him."
>
> Philip said to him, "Lord, show us the Father; that is all we need." Jesus answered, "For a long time I have been with you all; yet you do not know me, Philip? Whoever has seen me has seen the Father. Why, then, do you say, 'Show us the Father'? Do you not believe, Philip, that I am in the Father and the Father is in me?" (John 14:6–10).

Agnes Sanford used to say that Jesus is like a step-down transformer, because He renders the immeasurable power of God personally available to us.

So I urge men to draw closer to the Father God by getting to know Jesus. But I warn them that doing so ultimately brings them to the cross, which means death to the human self. To draw close to the Father through Jesus requires that a man give up all hope of ever receiving the love he needs from another human being. It means sacrificing at last the idols you have made of your "loved ones," and releasing those persons and those relationships to the Father for His cleansing and renewal.

Here is a sample prayer that I might invite a man to offer:

> Jesus, I thank You for laying down Your life so I could come even now to the Father through You.
>
> God, I confess that I have not known You as my Father. And so I have felt unloved for a long, long time. I need love, Father, and I know now that only You can give it to me. Forgive me for the times I've manipulated, threatened, or coerced other people to give me love—and the times I gave up altogether and just resented them, instead of turning to You.
>
> Jesus, I surrender to You. You are the way, the truth, and the life.
>
> Here I am, Father God, Your broken son. I need You, Father. Only You. Love me, Father.

Such a prayer offered in vulnerable openness and humility can be the first step in letting go of the parent, wife, child, or friend as an idol or source of saving love. It promises freedom in a man's relationships by releasing the other person at last from his or her role as the imagined savior.

Granted, when you go to Jesus and ask Him, as son to Father, for what you need, you may well feel like a child—but not as you did before, when you asked, begged, or demanded love from another human being. This time you will not be a child of the flesh, but a child of the Living God: weak and needy, true, but now surrendered to God and not to the self-centered human nature of yourself and others. In yielding to Jesus, a man can discover at last the love he longs for, as his now broken-open heart allows him to receive it.

Indeed, a man can realize that his Father God has only been waiting, even longing, for His beloved son to ask for His presence and love. As God declared of His "son" Israel, "I will take pleasure in doing good things for them" (Jer. 32:41). For doesn't a father enjoy doing good things for his son?

I once attended a conference in which Methodist evangelist Tommy Tyson delivered a stirring, joy-filled lesson. Later, Christian psychologist Judith MacNutt, speaking on the topic, "Finding the Father," noted Jesus' intimate relationship with the Father God, even calling him "Abba," or "Daddy." She then referred to Tyson: "Tommy's so joyful because he knows his Daddy loves him."

How many men today know Jesus well enough to say, "My Daddy loves me?"

More often a man projects onto God all the character flaws of his earthly father—perhaps the latter punished him harshly, abandoned him, judged or rejected him—and thus he cannot trust the Father God's loving overture in Jesus. Many men, in fact, have been so consistently disappointed by their father-in-the-flesh they will not even give God a chance to prove Himself.

Imagine being a loving father with the power to save your son in a threatening situation, but your son refuses to give you the chance to do it. Such a frustration portrays the Father God's reason for sending Jesus.

During the divided kingdom, Jerusalem was attacked by a united front of both Syrian and Israelite armies. King Ahaz became terrified and lost trust in God. The prophet Isaiah was sent to encourage him, but Ahaz was so afraid that he refused to give God a chance to prove His faithfulness. God declared that He would protect Ahaz, warning that "if your faith is not enduring, you will not endure." Then,

> The Lord sent another message to Ahaz: "Ask the Lord your God to give you a sign. It can be from deep in the world of the dead or from high up in heaven."
>
> Ahaz answered, "I will not ask for a sign. I refuse to put the Lord to the test."
>
> To that Isaiah replied, "Listen now, descendants of King David. It's bad enough for you to wear out the patience of men—do you have to wear out God's patience too? Well then, the Lord himself will give you a sign: a young woman who is pregnant will have a son and will name him 'Immanuel.' By the time he is old enough to make his own decisions, people will be eating milk and honey. Even before that time comes, the lands of the two kings who terrify you will be deserted" (Isa. 7:10–16).

Those men today who are willing to turn to Jesus and let God demonstrate His perfect love for them in "Immanuel," which means "God With Us," can discover at last what it means to know with heart and soul, "My Daddy loves me."

Furthermore, such men will discover something even greater than being loved, namely, loving. For one who has gone to the Source and received the Father's love is able to give it to others. John exhorts the followers of Jesus to "love one another" precisely because "love comes from God." The child of the flesh wants most to be loved; the child of God wants most to love, like the Father. And he knows he can do so only as he has drawn close to the Father through Jesus and received love to give.

When we have dared to become so child-like before God, we are freed to become more mature before other persons, ceasing to see them as parent-sources of love. Human nature is forever pulling petals off flowers to know whether the other "loves me or loves me not." But when you have gone to the Source and received the Father God's love for you, to be "in love" with someone else takes on new meaning. Then you know God has called you together to be a special channel for bringing His love to the other. It is not looking into each other's eyes; instead, it's seeing the other with the eyes of Jesus, and responding with compassion and truth spoken with love.

I once prayed, for example, with Gene, whose alcoholic father had belittled and abused him constantly as a boy. His wife also came from an alcoholic family, and so was struggling with considerable brokenness of her own. A Christian, Gene nevertheless found himself unable to respond to his wife's problems except with anger and resentment.

For several weeks, I worked with Gene to open him to the Father God's love—a difficult task, given his earthly father's rejection. First, he had to feel and cry out openly the pain his father had caused him. In doing so, he surrendered, and allowed Jesus to show him his father's own terrible, inner brokenness from hurts inflicted by Gene's father's father. At last, Gene forgave his father, and prayed for him. Then, soaked in mercy, Gene began to understand that the Father God loves both him and his earthly father.

Soon, Gene was ready to renounce his resentment toward his wife and exercise his proper authority as her husband—not to rule over her, but at last to seek with determination Jesus' saving power in her life.

I asked him if he were willing to let Jesus show him his wife as the Father God sees her?

He nodded, and I led him in prayer. As I laid a hand on Gene's shoulder and prayed quietly for him in the Spirit, I felt a sense of release.

"That's amazing!" Gene exclaimed suddenly.

"What?" I asked.

"As you began to pray, I saw her . . . it was strange . . . like she kind of shrank up from an adult woman into a little girl. She just got smaller, and as she did, she had her arms kind of around herself, like she was trying to hug herself or something." Gene paused. "She looked . . . awfully hurt and alone. . . ."

I invited Gene to hold that image of his wife and ask Jesus to go to her.

"It's funny . . . but as Jesus goes over to her, it's like I walk over with Him and . . . I can't tell if it's me or Him, but He's picking her up and holding her. . . ."

Gently, I explained to Gene that he had been interceding for his wife, and Jesus had shown him His intention for her. "Now where," I asked, tongue-in-cheek, "do you suppose Jesus could find someone to be His arms and heart of mercy for your wife like that?"

Gene smiled thinly and nodded, understanding. And then, together, we prayed for the right time when he might be the loving arms of Jesus to his wife.

Hence this prayer for all men: May we become so humble before our Father God in our own need, and so bold before others in His love, that we may indeed "love one another, because love comes from God."

12
Where Are All the Men?:
Why Men Don't Come to Church

"THE GREATEST DISAPPOINTMENT in my lifetime of ministry," a friend and fellow pastor in his late fifties once declared to me, "has been that I just never seem able to draw men into the church." He paused and sighed, confused and frustrated. "Sure, I've gotten males—but frankly, they've been mostly quiet and withdrawn guys with strong, dominant wives. I just wish I could get some *real* men in my church!" He grinned and shook his head in dismay. "At least, so I wouldn't have to be riding herd on all those strong women by myself!"

My association with fellow pastors over the years suggests that in his disappointment, my friend was speaking for a broad range of male clergy, both Catholic and protestant, liberal and conservative.

In fact, national parish consultant Dr. Lyle Schaller, in a briefing of United Methodist leaders, declared recently that the changing trend which "most concerns" him is the "feminization" of the church in "almost all denominations." He noted that in a general population of about 53 percent females and 47 percent males, Sunday worshipers are 60–62 percent female and only 38–40 percent male. Disturbed that "nobody is taking this seriously or attempting to find out why this is happening," Schaller challenged denominational leaders with the question, "Where are all the men?"[1]

In the parish I served for eight years, until 1985, those statistics were borne out. In fact, our 1985 records showed 63 percent of our active membership were women. Among those who were married, a full 25 percent worshiped without their husbands, who either never joined the church or chose after joining not to participate.

In those activities that directly reflect the ongoing life of the church—prayer, fellowship, and ministry to the community—the sex gap was worse than Schaller's most dire statistics. With a full 8 percent of our membership retired men, a weekday morning prayer and study group drew women only. A lunch-time group, scheduled to accommodate working persons, was all women. The after-worship time of prayer and sharing drew as many as ten women, but never more than two men besides myself. In gathering a lay "pastoral care committee" to visit and pray with the needy, I could identify only three men in the congregation who had demonstrated a concern for others' hurts and seemed comfortable praying with others; I could name a dozen women immediately. Our ministries to a local nursing home and a drug rehabilitation clinic drew only one male in each. The absence of men in these activities was not for lack of invitation or encouragement either from the pastor or others.

Shortly before my coming to the church, the board of deacons and the board of deaconesses had been merged into a single "diaconate," the constitution for which stipulated three men and three women. Each year the nominating committee struggled to find three qualified, motivated men; selecting the women was difficult only because there were so many from whom to choose.

Attempts to discover why men either do not come to

church, or come but do not participate, have prompted a variety of diagnoses.

Schaller himself speculates that perhaps the local congregation "usually offers women more entry points—places where they can become involved—than they offer men." Here I would ask, "What defines a particular church activity as an entry point for women and not men?" With the exception of women's fellowship groups, I know of no mainline church that excludes men from worship, prayer groups, fellowship events, committees, or other activities. Schaller is probably saying simply that to attract men, a church should offer activities in which men are already more comfortable and customarily more involved—perhaps even on Sunday mornings, when they are not in church. The logical extreme of this idea would be a large TV screen on the altar for football games, or mechanical challenges such as cars and computers to be worked on in the sanctuary or church parking lot.

While such extremes are foolish, I am quite certain that many churches, in their desperation to attract men, have resorted to the same basic logic. When in my first year at the church I sought to start a men's fellowship, I asked some of the older men what programs had drawn male support in the past. Several recalled with enthusiasm a men's fellowship evening in the church recreation hall when one man had shown films of the latest jet fighter planes. "That was the best turnout for men that I can ever remember for a church function," one said. "We really enjoyed that."

I felt torn inside. On the one hand, the topic of jet fighter planes clearly met those men where they were at that time and drew their attendance and enthusiasm. But X-rated movies would likely have done the same. Jesus, who healed bodies and blessed "the peacemakers" while urging His followers to "turn the other cheek," surely cannot be comfortable with fighter-plane movies, any more than X-rated ones. Yet men clearly followed Jesus—real men, strong enough to haul heavy fishing nets every day of their lives. Jesus did meet men where they were, but only to lead them where they needed to go. Apparently no one at that most popular men's fellowship meeting had led the men beyond their enthusiasm for war machines.

Every other organization for men judges its programs by how well they carry out its purpose. A men's softball team, for example, does not recruit men by showing movies of warplanes. It simply says, "We are a softball team. If you want to play softball, join us." The organization is predicated on the "faith" that the desire to play softball exists in enough men to draw them out and form a team.

Can we Christians simply dare to tell men, "We are the Body of Christ. If you want to know Jesus Christ, receive His power, and do His work in this world, join us"? Or are we afraid that the desire to know Jesus and do His work is just not in enough men to warrant forming His church? Biblical faith understands that God "created the world" (Heb. 1:2) through Jesus. So the desire to know Jesus Christ must exist in all of God's creation—including men—no matter how deeply hidden.

Why, then, are our churches so unsuccessful in bringing forth that desire in men?

One diagnosis for the lack of men in church is that God is presented as "Father." And today, in our culture, the human father is often absent from the home, either away at work or divorced from the mother and living elsewhere. Denied the necessary masculine care of his father, a boy develops negative associations with the role of "father," and transfers those negative feelings toward God as "Father." So he avoids God, and therefore, the church.

But if this argument holds for boys, it should hold for girls, too. If the father is absent from the home, he is absent from the daughter as well as from the son, and those daughters should also have the same negative associations with "father" and should project those onto God and the church. But the women *do* come to church. Could it be that those women who were not loved by their fathers come to church to gain that love from the Father-God? If so, then why are the men not coming to church, for the same reason? The brother is just as hurt by the father's neglect as the sister. What compels the female to seek the Father-God's love in church while the male stays away?

In desperation we say, "If only we had more men in church already, that would attract other men." While this might well be true, it doesn't help us understand why we don't have more men there in the first place.

One helpful source is a *Challenge to Evangelism Today* interview with Dr. Donald M. Joy of Asbury Theological Seminary titled, "Is The Church Feminized?" Responding directly to Dr. Schaller's earlier question, Joy emphasizes that, because so many fathers are emotionally absent from their sons, "the deformed male is now emerging as the 'norm'" in our society. The tough "macho" image is designed to compensate for this insecurity, and it becomes "not macho to be in church."

As an example of "healthy masculinity," Joy points to "a high investment in the care of the young," citing again the messianic prophecy in which God promises first to send Elijah, who "will bring fathers and children together again" (Mal. 4:5). Connecting this to the strong preaching on repentance by John the Baptist, who "will go on before the Lord, in the spirit and power of Elijah, to turn the hearts of the fathers to their children" (Luke 1:15–17), Joy declares that "The hope for our generation . . . (is) that men who are practicing repentance as a way of life will find their hearts turn toward their children."

Specifically, Joy calls men to "an orientation toward perpetual repentance for our unbridled toughness, our tendency to control everything, our chauvinism, our frightening impatience with our children, our tendency to pride and arrogance." He concludes:

> For most of us, that kind of daily surrender is the key to honesty in all relationships, and it comes at a high price. Interestingly enough, these tamed men love the parts they can contribute to their homes by active parenting. And healthy males and females are what will make Lyle Schaller's fears of the feminized church go away. Men whose hearts are turned toward their children will be transforming our churches, doing the work of the Bridegroom who gives his life for his Bride—the Church.[2]

Certainly, Joy offers an attractive vision. We all want to see more psychologically healthy males in our society. Anyone who has ever been a boy wants to see more fathers willing to show love and care for their sons. But just because a man is psychologically healthy and a caring father does not mean he will go to a church, much less be willing to work at "transforming" it. We simply have no guarantee that today's caring father will not be out fishing or playing ball with his son on Sunday morning instead of taking him to church.

Something about Joy's image of the "tamed" male hints of one-sidedness. It's entirely focused on men's becoming more feminized in outlook and behavior. Certainly, to the extent that we men have avoided and even scorned such "feminine" virtues as child-nurturing, we need to become more feminized. But this is nothing new; we have been hearing it since the sexual revolution of the sixties, and heeding it to a surprising degree.

The question is not whether men should be "tamed," for any unbridled lack of discipline ultimately harms others and keeps one from accomplishment in one's own life. The question, rather, is "tamed by whom, and to what order?" The current lack of male participation in our churches seems clear testimony that men will not be tamed by a program based exclusively upon feminine virtues.

Anyone who doubts that men want to be tamed at all simply has not observed young men marching in military uniform. Despite the expected complaints against military restriction, the young man takes great masculine pride in obeying his commander's orders. He clearly recognizes the discipline, structure, and focus of the military as essential to manhood. In military service, a man not only agrees to submit to authority, but indeed he longs for it as an opportunity to demonstrate proper manly restraint.

Nor is this sense of military authority and obedience counter to the Kingdom of God. When God rules, we live under His authority and must know how to obey. For so the Roman officer impressed Jesus when the officer's slave was dying and he sought Jesus' healing:

> "I do not deserve to have you come into my house, neither do I consider myself worthy to come to you in person. Just give the order, and my servant will get well. I, too, am a man placed under

the authority of superior officers, and I have soldiers under me. I order this one, 'Go!' and he goes; I order that one, 'Come!' and he comes; and I order my slave 'Do this!' and he does it."

Jesus was surprised when he heard this; he turned around and said to the crowd following him, "I tell you, I have never found faith like this, not even in Israel!" (Luke 7:6–9).

The church has done much over the centuries to encourage men to pursue feminine virtues. But we have not sought and portrayed Christ-centered ways to pursue masculine virtues. It is not enough for Christians to portray weakness and tenderness as acceptable in a man. We also must portray the manly strength and firmness that is of God. We must demonstrate that weakness confessed and submitted to the Living God through Jesus Christ ultimately brings the very masculine strength for which men hunger: toughness in the face of opposition, decisiveness in the face of uncertainty, and saving power in the face of danger.

The church which ignores or even scorns such masculine values must ultimately lose all men and become wholly feminized; the church which accedes to the worldly definition of those values must lose Jesus Christ and become wholly secularized. The options then become either the church and no men, or the men and no church.

The work of God among men today—and so, the work of the Church—is not to feminize our masculinity, but to redeem it, not to make men more like women, but to make us more authentic men. Certainly, authentic masculinity includes such "feminine" components as tenderness and nurturing care. But a man cannot duly embrace his "feminine side" without first being grounded firmly in his masculine foundation. Without that, tenderness and nurturing care in the man too easily become fearful accommodation to the other person, and abandonment of his manly courage and strength.

Toughness, for example, is essential in the effort to bring God's kingdom to this broken earth as it is in heaven. As Dr. Joy says, we men do need to repent of our "unbridled toughness"— not, however, to become exclusively meek, but so that our toughness might be "bridled" to serve God's purposes and not our own. Jesus was tough when He stood up to the Pharisees, to the mob about to stone the adulteress, to the Gerasene demoniac, and even to the hysterical crowd of relatives who gathered after the death of the synagogue president's daughter:

> Then Jesus went into the official's house. When he saw the musicians for the funeral and the people all stirred up, he said, "Get out, everybody! The little girl is not dead—she is only sleeping!" Then they all started making fun of him. But as soon as the people had been put out, Jesus went into the girl's room and took hold of her hand, and she got up (Matt. 9:23–25).

Imagine if Jesus had meekly acceded to the feelings of everyone there, and not been tough enough to stand His ground and send them away at such an emotionally precarious time. He could have backed away gently from the whole thing—and the girl would have remained dead.

Clearly, we men must repent not for our toughness *per se*, but rather, for its "unbridled" character at times. Toughness submitted to Jesus and exercised for God's purposes is an essential Christian virtue. Too often, however, Christians allow the inference that toughness itself is a sin by failing to portray and affirm a redeemed toughness in God's service. This is what drives men away from the church, for it seems to condemn manliness as a sin.

So the church today is perceived by men as a feminine bridle upon their toughness. Small wonder, then, that they reject it. But the only bridle that can legitimately be offered to men is the one offered by God Himself in Jesus Christ, who urged, "Take my yoke and put it on you, and learn from me, because I am gentle and humble in spirit; and you will find rest. For the yoke I will give you is easy, and the load I will put on you is light" (Matt. 10:29, 30).

As Episcopalian Terry Fullam has noted of this text, when two animals are yoked, the way is "easy" only if the two are going in the same direction. If we are going in Jesus' direction, he carries the burden and we simply follow; if we pull against Jesus, intending to go our own direction, we struggle under a considerable burden.

Authentic Christian manhood, therefore, is manifested only in the man tamed by the Living God—the man who has offered himself as a "living sacrifice" (Rom. 12:1) to the Father through Jesus Christ and who is thereby empowered not by his own strength, but by the Holy Spirit. Doctrines and creeds may be trail markers along the way, but they cannot substitute for Jesus, who alone *is* the way. For He alone is the authentic man, the new Adam who is wholly tamed by God and who cannot be subdued by the powers of the world:

> Adam was a figure of the one who was to come. . . . Just as all people were made sinners as the result of the disobedience of one man (Adam), in the same way they will all be put right with God as the result of the obedience of the one man (Jesus) (Rom. 5:14b, 19).

Therefore, the true Christian man is, by the nature of his origin and calling, an outlaw in this world, much like Abraham and the other ancient faith witnesses who "admitted openly that they were foreigners and refugees on earth" (Heb. 11:13). As Jesus declared, "I have not come to call respectable people, but outcasts" (Matt. 9:13). The powers of the world must therefore fear the man of God, criticizing and attacking him. To the man of God, this opposition is not a warning; it is an authenticating promise. In fact, Jesus reserves His warning not for those who are persecuted by the world, but for those who are not: "How terrible when all people speak well of you; their ancestors said the very same things about the false prophets" (Luke 6:26). The most profound criticism I ever heard of a Christian—in this case a nationally known church leader—was that "he's never done anything that might get him crucified."

Like the true warrior, the man of God does not operate under "civilian" law. Certainly, he may suffer its consequences, as Jesus did on the Cross; but he is ultimately accountable only to the higher law of his Commander. In obedience to God, he is as likely to be protesting nonviolently at a nuclear arms facility as laying hands on a sick person and praying for healing, as likely to be speaking out at a well-to-do city council meeting in behalf of senior-citizen housing as fasting and praying alone.

An essential part of God's manliness cannot accommodate the world; the man of God cannot be domesticated. This unsettled-ness of the masculine is no less than the Father's discontent with the world's manmade replacements for His order. Such holy restlessness is granted to those whom God has called to restore His kingdom to this world: it is granted to the men. Indeed, the root meaning of the world "holy" is "set apart," that is, belonging to God and not to the world: "You shall be holy and belong only to me, because I am the Lord and I am holy. I have set you apart from the other nations so that you would belong to me alone" (Lev. 20:26).

Most men sense this restlessness within themselves. Lacking spiritual understanding, however, they misinterpret it as a license to copout on commitment and responsibility and become a romantic "rambler," who refuses to be "tied down" by woman, job, or locale. The world, of course, rushes in to fill the vacuum created by our spiritual abdication, substituting its own images of "masculine boldness" in those who break God's law to serve their own ends: the slick thief, the tough mafia murderer, the clever adulterer. Simply to denounce such images as antisocial or even ungodly cannot overcome their power to woo men. In addition, Christians must proclaim God's discontent with the world's order and portray the authentic man of God as one who acts against that order—not to gratify his own selfish desires, but to re-establish the intended order of God's kingdom on earth.

Boldness, according to the world, belongs to the man who fears neither God nor other men; for Christians, boldness belongs to the man who fears God more than any other man—or woman (Luke 12:4, 5).

In this understanding of boldness, Jesus can be seen as the "Iron Hans" who cannot be restrained by the power of any earthly king or authority. He allows Himself to be captured on the cross by men precisely so that He might capture men in their own brokenness. Like the law-giver Moses before Him, Jesus calls men into the self-defeating ordeal of the wilderness, away from their slavery to the world's values, in order to make them sons of God, warriors in His kingdom.

My goal in this book is not to offer yet another guide for helping men "embrace our feminine side," nor to become more socialized by the world's standards. Rather, I want to encourage men to follow Jesus: to be crucified to self and resurrected in His image in order to embrace our true manly courage and strength— and then to transform this world "on earth as it is in heaven."

Without such a model inside the church, I am convinced it is far better for a son to be out in the woods with his father than in church with his mother alone. Yet God certainly cannot settle for an "either-or" in this case, and neither must we in the church. For a son needs his father to guide him to both emotional *and* spiritual fellowship. Why not fish together on Saturday *and* worship together on Sunday? Clearly, the lack of such a model among us suggests that men simply do not recognize spiritual reality and the human need for a relationship with the God who defines it.

For example, in Dr. Lee Salk's recent book, *My Father, My Son*, twenty-eight father-son relationships are described in the first person, and not a single father or son mentions religious faith at all. Even in the most tender, loving, and mutually affirming of these accounts—"My father loved his family and showed it"—no father gives any indication that he desires religious faith for himself or his son. Today's father who says, "I want to show my son love," may never even think of taking the boy to church, especially if church is not something the father already values for himself.

Again, the problem cannot be solved by urging mothers to bring their sons to church with them, for ultimately the boy looks to the father for manly identity. In *Trial by Fire*, Anne White notes the biblical exhortation,

> Fathers, do not provoke your children to anger, but bring them up in the discipline and instruction of the Lord (Eph. 6:4 RSV).

She declares that this standard,

. . . has too often been neglected by fathers who provided well for their children's physical needs and abominably for their spiritual and emotional needs! Although the wife can most certainly be delegated this authority by her husband, if it is a "cop out" (an escape from responsibility) on his part, the child will know the difference. If the father does not consider important his spiritual leadership of his home, his children will ultimately decide that the Lord is not very important or that "religion is sissy stuff." How many mothers know with a broken heart that their teen-age sons are listening more to their father's lack of faith than to their mother's words or acts of faith—in homes where the father is not a Christian and the mother's "walk in the light" is a lonely one. These children are "spiritually and emotionally deprived"—regardless of the financial and intellectual or cultural adequacy of their homes.[3]

Here we must confront a final, and perhaps more enduring theory of why men stay away from church: is church for sissies? What can Christians tell men about an organization whose Founder gives blessings to those who "mourn . . . are humble . . . are merciful to others . . . pure in heart . . . work for peace . . . (and) are persecuted" (Matt. 5:3–10)? How are we to explain a spokesman who confessed that his value to the organization lay in his "weaknesses" (2 Cor. 12:9)?

First, we must challenge the assumption that any organization which stresses humility, weakness, and brokenness is doomed to fail in attracting men. Consider, for example, one well-known international voluntary organization which draws a large percentage of men even though it struggles against a favorite aspect of the popular macho lifestyle. It's called Alcoholics Anonymous, and its program says that you don't have to drink to be manly, indeed, that drinking can be a sign of crippling inner weaknesses.

From the outset, the A.A. program refutes popular masculine images. In its first three "steps" members declare,

1. We admitted we were powerless over alcohol—that our lives had become unmanageable.
2. Came to believe that a Power greater than ourselves could restore us to sanity.

3. Made a decision to turn our will and our lives over to the care of God *as we understood Him.*[4]

A.A. does not show jet-fighter-plane movies or plan sports outings to attract men. Unlike most churches, it does not invest energies into offering a large variety of activities to attract or accommodate those who otherwise might not want to join. There is just one door into A.A.: a desire to stop drinking, and to live a new life.

And the men come. Many men. Men who might otherwise be drinking with buddies or watching a football game go to A.A. meetings instead. What's more, they do un-macho things like share their needs openly before others, and even join hands and pray together at the end of the meeting.

A.A. knows what it is, and what it offers. It does no advertising, but relies solely on its reputation for doing what it says. It knows that its program is effective only when the person wants it—not simply because the wife or mother wants it for him. A.A. has no time to worry over the "feminization" of the organization; it is too busy doing its job, ministering to the men who are already there in great numbers.

Perhaps not surprisingly, A.A. urges those who would help alcoholics to adopt a stance of "tough love," that is, not to cover up for the alcoholic, but to confront him or her directly with the effects of his or her drinking and enforce the consequences. Love without this toughness, A.A. says, only encourages the other person to continue drinking.

The ability of A.A. to attract men should prompt a profound embarrassment among churchmen, for it reveals our own unwillingness to wield the manly sword of truth ourselves—to be honest about our own brokenness and tough with one another. In fact, the A.A. Twelve-Step Program is taken directly from a basic Christian conversion plan developed in the last century and based upon Romans 7. But A.A. prohibits the mention of Jesus or any other specific religion, to preclude any sense of judgment or exclusivity.

I believe that God raised up A.A. as a second-best alternative to His church, because it proclaims both forgiveness and redemption. But because it does not proclaim Jesus, A.A. is handicapped by its inability to embrace the Source and sustaining Power of its program. It can chart the first steps toward manly truth; but the task remains for the Church, the Body of Christ, to draw men into the fullness of manhood, empowered by courage and strength from the Father God.

We Christian men must be willing, even eager, to say to others, "We are men who have come face-up against our personal brokenness, and discovered it to be so deep and so intrinsic that we cannot by our own efforts overcome it. We have found that only by turning our lives over to Jesus Christ do we gain courage and strength to be the men we want to be."

Surely, the Church of Jesus Christ can and must demonstrate such bold self-honesty, as A.A. does, and trust that other men do indeed need the Lord and the fellowship in Him that we offer. Surely, we must minister to the men already among us in the church, and be willing to pray and wait for those who have not yet realized they need the Body of Christ.

The example of A.A. shows that those who do their job well don't have to wait long.

13

Rational and Independent,
Faithless and Alone

IN OUR SECULAR SOCIETY, men are understood to be created not in the image of God, but in the image of the world—which the media readily reflect. And perhaps no media image has so deeply affected our male self-image as that of the cowboy, whose major characteristics can be inferred from the popular country-western song, "Mamas, Don't Let Your Babies Grow Up to Be Cowboys." Sung by Willie Nelson, the most popular proponent of the "outlaw" lifestyle, the song is a tongue-in-cheek warning that actually exalts the cowboy image.

The song's list of what "cowboys like," ranges from puppies and poolrooms to children and "girls of the night." Conspicuously absent from the list is another adult in an ongoing relationship with the cowboy. The following verses comprise an anthem to masculine alienation, declaring how hard cowboys are to love— even "harder to hold." Indeed, the song concludes with a pathetic epitaph declaring that even when they're with those they love, cowboys are "always alone."

This "lone ranger" model of manhood, pervasive in our culture, is rooted in isolation so deeply and so hopelessly that separation from other persons is proclaimed a virtue, as if to say, "We have no idea how to overcome our alienation from others, so rather than face its underlying brokenness and be emotionally destroyed, we will pretend it is noble and right."

A more middle-class version of this male effort to disparage community in order to avoid the pain of alienation was Frank Sinatra's self-tailored song, "I Did It My Way." Here, the singer exalts the rugged individualism of his past and can now "face the final curtain" of his life feeling proud—yet also hollow and empty, lacking the comfort and joy of another human being—or God—whose "way" might have helped, or even saved him.

Significantly, these songs do not proclaim simple independence from the woman—which might in some cases be temporarily healthy—but rather, alienation from all other persons, including other men. Pathology lurks here. As author David Smith, in *The Friendless American Male*, records one man's explanation: "Of course I don't have friends. I'm a man. My wife is the one with friends."[1] In our culture, women are perceived as the ones who sustain relationships. When a marriage falters, the wife is far more likely to seek help first; wives write the Christmas cards and the personal letters to "our friends." They arrange the family social events. Men often patronize women for their "gabbing," but in our hearts we see in it what we miss ourselves: that *communication* and *community* share the same root word.

Here at last, we are ready to portray the fundamental rub between men and church.

Jesus outlined the two basic foundations of His call when He answered the question, "Which is the greatest commandment in the Law?" For He could not affirm number one without at the same time affirming number two:

"Love the Lord your God with all your heart, with all your soul, and with all your mind." This is the greatest and most important commandment. The second most important commandment is like it: "Love your neighbor as yourself." The whole law of Moses and the teachings of the prophets depend on these two commandments (Matt. 22:36–40).

Clearly, the faith of Jesus—and those who would follow Him—rests upon relationship with God and relationship with other persons. The very earliest church embodied this orientation in its daily activities. Just after the church had been born through the coming of the Holy Spirit, the newly baptized believers "spent their time in learning from the apostles, taking part in the fellowship, and sharing in the fellowship meals and the prayers" (Acts 2:42). Prayer and fellowship were central to the earliest identity of the Christian Church: prayer, to nurture relationship with God, and fellowship, to nurture relationship with one another. The "learning" or "Christian education" kept the prayer and fellowship true to God's intent. And in a marvelous mystery, the *commun*ion meal melded and celebrated the believer's fellowship with both the Lord and His Body, the *commun*ity of faith.

And so Jesus declared that loving fellowship with God "is like" loving fellowship with one another. The early church considered the two so central to the faith as to be mutually dependent:

> If someone says he loves God but hates his brother, he is a liar. For he cannot love God, whom he has not seen, if he does not love his brother, whom he has seen. The command that Christ has given us is this: whoever loves God must love his brother also (1 John 4:20, 21).

Again, Jesus addresses The Lord's Prayer to "Our Father," not "My Father." Even as He teaches His people to communicate with God, Jesus establishes community as basic and essential.

Often, however, I have heard men protest that they do not need to go to church to pray with others, because they "feel closer to God" when they are "in God's great outdoors," while fishing, hunting, or playing golf. Certainly, nature reflects the glory of its Creator God. Even the most ancient pagan religions saw divine presence in nature; indeed, they held up the sky, sun, earth, and other parts of nature as gods themselves. What makes the Christian faith unique is that we believe God has revealed Himself not primarily in the sky and earth, but in a human named "Jesus."

Our ancient, pagan ancestors worshiped nature. But a Christian man knows that a sunset, no matter how beautiful, cannot heal the hurts inflicted upon him by others; a forest, no matter how majestic, cannot overcome his selfish pride and show him his true purpose in life; an ocean full of fish, no matter how stirring, cannot help him hear the cries of broken fellow human beings and give him power to help them. Only God, through the broken body of Christ and His Holy Spirit—manifested today in the church— can do these things.

In seeking to share this idea with male parishioners, I have struggled against an inner fear of backlash, as have many wives who "bring their husbands to church." The man might respond, "You should be glad that I at least come to church occasionally with my family, even if I don't pray or want any relationship with God or the others there."

But how can I be glad when someone has cut himself off from life itself, from his very Creator and fellow creatures?

Indeed, in the earliest church "all the believers continued together in *close* fellowship" (Acts 2:44 italics added). Clearly, the Church of Jesus Christ is comprised of "believers," not those who come simply to be with their families. Furthermore, the scripture notes that fellowship in the body of believers requires—no, let us proclaim it: *promises*—"sharing" in "the common life" together— even unto your total "belongings" (v. 43). The promise of God through Jesus in the Holy Spirit is that we no longer need to fear closeness with one another, as a burden; instead we can celebrate it as a gift and rely upon it as the major context for God's saving power in our lives.

The interdependent warp and woof of the church life-fabric are therefore spirituality—that is, relationship with God, as through prayer, worship, and Bible study—and community, our relationship with one another through close fellowship. We in the Christian Church are therefore a spiritual community, people gathered because the God who "is Spirit" (John 4:24) has called us together. And we proclaim a communal spirituality, one discerned, cultivated, and brought to loving service only together with others in close fellowship.

Clearly, those who are oriented toward a life of both spirituality and community—who value spiritual reality and enjoy sharing intimately with others—will be drawn to the Christian Church. On the other hand, those who are oriented about a life of physical/rational reality and individuality—who value human power and independence from others—will not.

From this perspective, a feminine orientation is far more amenable to the biblical understanding of church life than a masculine.

To answer the original question, "Where are all the men?" we must ask the more basic question, "What in the male makeup or experience biases men away from spirituality and community and toward natural human power and independence?"

A credible answer to this new question might be as follows:

We value/incline ourselves toward those endeavors which most affirm ourselves. Men, being stronger physically and more dominant in the worldly power structures of politics, economics, and religious organizations, tend to be more physically and rationally oriented. We devalue and withdraw from power which threatens to overshadow our own; hence, men withdraw from supra-human, supra-natural spiritual power. And finally, when one's own individual power is being affirmed, the community simply serves no useful purpose; "I did it my way," as Frank Sinatra proclaimed, becomes gospel. Women, on the other hand, being so long denied access to worldly power structures, naturally turn to seek power elsewhere—indeed, seek any power which is more universally available and promises in fact to be greater than the power wielded by the male-dominated world. Furthermore, women may be drawn into community simply out of protection, being vulnerable to male-dominated worldly power.

Clearly, Christianity fills the bill precisely for such a female search. Its power is universally available to women as well as men:

> This is what I will do in the last days, God says: I will pour out my
> Spirit on everyone. Your sons and daughters will proclaim my
> message. . . . Yes, even on my servants, both men and women, I
> will pour out my Spirit . . . (Acts 2:17–18).

And this power of Christianity exceeds that of the world: "The
Spirit who is in you is more powerful than the spirit in those who
belong to the world" (1 John 4:4).

This argument that men, who enjoy the world's physical, rational power, are threatened by and thus denigrate spiritual power,
is compelling—at least with respect to white, Western males, who
wield such worldly power.

Such a power-centered model may explain the Western
male's aversion to spirituality, but it does not account for our aversion to community. Simply enjoying the world's physical, rational
power would not require one to eschew fellowship. We might
therefore ask whether some unique aspect of the male experience
could mitigate against men's seeing themselves in relation to any
one besides themselves—even to God.

In her ground-breaking book, *In a Different Voice*, Harvard
professor of education Carol Gilligan outlines a basic difference
between the male and female infant experience, and how that
shapes adult orientation toward life. Gilligan notes a 1974 study
by sociologist Nancy Chodorow which attributes male-female differences not to anatomy, but to the fact that "women, universally,
are largely responsible for early child care," when the basic core
personality is formed. Mothers, Chodorow says, "tend to experience their daughters as more like, and continuous with, themselves." A girl's identity, therefore, is formed in the "experience of
attachment."

On the other hand, "mothers experience their sons as male
opposite." The boy, in an effort to identify himself as masculine,
must therefore separate from the mother and cut off his "primary
love and sense of empathic tie." As Chodorow summarizes,

> (G)irls emerge with a stronger basis for experiencing another's
> needs or feelings as one's own . . . from very early, then, because

they are parented by a person of the same gender. . . . (G)irls come to experience themselves as less differentiated than boys, as more continuous with and related to the external object world, and as differently oriented to their inner-object world as well.[2]

Consequently, Gilligan concludes,

. . . relationships, and particularly issues of dependency, are experienced differently by women and men. For boys and men, separation and individuation are critically tied to gender identity since separation from the mother is essential for the development of masculinity. For girls and women, issues of femininity or feminine identity do not depend on the achievement of separation from the mother or on the progress of individuation. Since masculinity is defined through separation while feminity is defined through attachment, male gender identity is threatened by intimacy while female gender identity is threatened by separation. Thus males tend to have difficulty with relationships, while females tend to have problems with individuation.[3]

Here, then, is the crux of the matter. For life in the church of Jesus Christ focuses entirely upon "relationships, and particularly issues of dependency"—relationships with God and with one another, and dependency upon God and one another. If for males the thrust of maturing to manhood is in the direction of "separation and individuation," then clearly the church and males are moving in opposite directions from the very outset— and the issue of conversion to a Christian life-orientation is far more complex and demanding for men than for women. Indeed, if the church is marching like a mighty army to reestablish God's kingdom on earth through spirituality and community, then the cowboys—and the legions of males who ride with them in their life-orientation—are at best beating a retreat, and at worst, serving in the enemy's army.

If Gilligan's insight is true, that men perceive relationship *per se* as a threat to masculine identity out of a primal need to individuate from the mother, then that country-western song which focuses on the relationship between cowboys and their mothers becomes remarkably apt, as "Mamas, Don't Let Your Babies Grow Up to Be Cowboys."

The focus of the cowboy's life-orientation is the mama who would restrain the male baby from separation/individuation and thus impel him toward such extreme alienation as described in the song, in order to wrest himself from the mother's grasp. "Mamas" are portrayed as having the power to hand their sons over to further communal involvement, symbolized by "doctors and lawyers and such"—who have more interpersonal contact than the more lone, individual job of truck-driving. Again, the song urges mothers not to let their sons "pick guitars"—an instrument designed more to play alone than with others.

Certainly, most middle-class men whose lives are invested in families, neighborhoods, and regular jobs may cherish the cowboy fantasy even when they know they cannot live it out. Anxious to flee relationships, while knowing he must have them to maintain the security of home and job, a man may simply abdicate to his wife the job of sustaining relationships, to save face. Thus the woman writes the cards and letters, handles family social events, intercedes in quarrels, and goes to church— serving as the maker and sustainer of relationships in behalf of the man.

The man who dares to appreciate the woman's doing this must face the fact that he has allowed the woman to do something for him that he has refused to do for himself. He thereby remains in the boy-mother mode. Ultimately, the man must resent the woman for co-opting the very independent, self-reliant task of developing for himself the relationships he needs. This resentment is heightened when he begins to realize that these relationships form a wholly new, and thus frightening arena for him. He recognizes that the woman is braver than he is in that arena, and so his enforced alienation ultimately becomes a block to the very independence and self-esteem he seeks.

Since our Creator has designed us to function properly only in relationship to Him and to one another, sooner or later the need for relationship will surface in every man. As long as he hides that need behind the woman, she is only too happy to assume the power and superiority from which the man has withdrawn. For example, country-western singer Tammy Wynette's seventies hit, "Stand By Your Man," betrayed a patronizing tone as it called the woman to let her man "cling to" her when lonely, and to "be proud" of him because, "after all, he's just a man." Significantly, shortly after recording "Stand By Your Man," Wynette left her husband and recorded a new hit, "D-I-V-O-R-C-E."

In an earlier day, when divorce was not so acceptable, men sometimes negotiated a trade-off, saying to the woman, "As long as you keep me in relationship to other people and God, I'll keep you in the house, car, food, and clothing." But with the flood of today's women into the job world, such a trade-off carries less value from the working woman's point of view. Even as women have dared to move into the economic marketplace, so men today must dare to move into deliberate relationships.

Neither man nor woman may be wholly comfortable in this new "place." But the new strength which such a challenge brings to each of us can only strengthen our relationships with each other.

In fact, as women begin more often to work outside the home, they no longer have the time or energy to bear the entire responsibility for spiritual leadership in the family. The time is therefore ripe today for men at last to step in and assume their proper role of spiritual leadership.

Meanwhile, the women may need for their own spiritual growth to take jobs and participate more in worldly power. For one can affirm spiritual power only after participating enough in worldly power to discover its limitations. It is one level of faith to affirm spiritual power because you have no other power available, but a deeper level to have participated in worldly power and chosen to affirm God's power as supreme. You first must *have* worldly power before you can yield it to God.

As part of their faith journey women may have to taste enough economic and political power to discover its ultimate emptiness and then eventually to reembrace spiritual power with a more authentic commitment. Until reaching that point, women will be tempted to wield spiritual power as a weapon in the flesh, disparaging men's worldly power simply out of their own self-centered disappointment at not having it themselves. Ironically, the man may be in a better position today to affirm spirituality because he has experienced secularity deeply enough to know its ultimate limitation.

In many ways men have exercised their natural human power in the church—so convincingly that many might wonder how it could possibly be viewed as "feminized." After all, aren't most clergy and church officials male? Don't men write its systematic theology?

But such questions actually illustrate the distinction between religion, which preserves the stories and principles upon which the faith is based, and spirituality, which reencounters the faith experience to which the stories and principles witness. Clearly, natural human power can accomplish religion, but not spirituality. That is why men are more comfortable with religion than with spirituality.

We are most anxious to control what we most fear. One who fears relationship will therefore try to control his or her relationship with God as well as with other persons. Men most commonly do this through systems of law and institutional hierarchies, which reduce relationship to some manageable form. Similarly, we men may seek to allay our fear of a Living God by writing elaborate "systematic theologies," believing we can use those theologies to keep the "hound of heaven" on a leash of rationality.

Gilligan traces this urge to the male infant's struggle to separate from the mother while longing to stay at her breast for comfort and nourishment:

> This disengagement of self from the world outside, however, initiates not only the process of differentiation but also the search for autonomy, the wish to gain control over the sources and objects of pleasure in order to shore up the possibilities for happiness against the risk of disappointment and loss. Thus connection—associated by Freud with "infantile helplessness" and "limitless narcissism," with illusion and the denial of danger—gives way to separation. Consequently, assertion, linked to aggression, becomes the basis for relationships. In this way, a primary separation, arising from disappointment and fueled by rage, creates a self

whose relations with others or "objects" must then be protected by rules, a morality that contains this explosive potential and adjusts "the mutual relationships of human beings in the family, the state and the society" (Freud).[4]

In a fascinating study of male behavior, Gilligan quotes an experiment by sociologist Janet Lever, who observed fifth-grade boys and girls in their respective recess games. Lever discovered that the boys' games invariably lasted longer than the girls', because when a difference of opinion came up, the boys were "able to resolve the disputes more effectively than the girls":

> During the course of this study, boys were seen quarreling all the time, but not once was a game terminated because of a quarrel and no game was interrupted for more than seven minutes. In the gravest debates, the final word was always, to "repeat the play," generally followed by a chorus of "cheaters' proof." In fact, it seemed that the boys enjoyed the legal debates as much as they did the game itself, and even marginal players of lesser size or skill participated equally in these recurrent squabbles. In contrast, the eruption of disputes among girls tended to end the game.[5]

That is, the girls "subordinated the continuation of the game to the continuation of relationships." Gilligan then quotes a study in this context by Jean Piaget, and concludes,

> Girls are more tolerant in their attitudes toward rules, more willing to make exceptions, and more easily reconciled to innovations. As a result, the legal sense, which Piaget considers essential to moral development, "is far less developed in little girls than in boys."[6]

This basic male urge to control relationships by rules has profound and indeed, ominous implications for the church, for it undermines the very heart of the gospel. Jesus came to destroy the prison of law into which men had locked their relationships with God and one another. As Paul emphasized to the Romans, the very reason for joining the Body of Christ is to receive and act out that freedom:

That is the way it is with you, my brothers. You have also died, as far as the Law is concerned, because you are part of the Body of Christ; and now you belong to him who was raised from death in order that we might be useful in the service of God. For when we lived according to our human nature, the sinful desires stirred up in us by the Law were at work in our bodies, and we were useful in the service of death. Now, however, we are free from the Law, because we died to that which once held us prisoners. No longer do we serve in the old way of a written law, but in the new way of the Spirit (7:4–6).

And again, to the Galatians:

Freedom is what we have—Christ has set us free! Stand, then, as free men, and do not become slaves again. . . . If the Spirit leads you, then you are not subject to the Law (5:1, 18).

The new covenant in Christ, Paul explains to the Corinthians, is not like the old covenant in Moses:

There is nothing in us that allows us to claim that we are capable of doing this work. The capacity we have comes from God; it is he who made us capable of serving the new covenant, which consists not of a written law, but of the Spirit. The written law brings death, but the Spirit gives life (2 Cor. 3:5–6).

Jesus, then, is the new covenant, the new law—the Living God present with His people "always, to the end of the age" (Matt. 28:20). His death on the Cross enabled God to send the same Holy Spirit which had guided and empowered Jesus now to fill His body, the church, with every gift of knowledge, discernment, and word of God necessary to know God's will and act accordingly (1 Cor. 12).

Life in the Holy Spirit of the Living God—not the written law—was the hallmark of life in the earliest Body of Christ. And the Spirit is not something which men can bind up and control by their own laws. Indeed, as Jesus declared to Nicodemus, the leader of the Pharisees, "The wind blows where it wishes; you hear the sound it makes, but you do not know where it comes from or where it is going. It is the same way with everyone who is born of the Spirit (John 3:8).

So what sort of person is best suited to this life in the Holy Spirit, which is the essence of life in the Church? Clearly, not the boys, who are busy trying to be "protected by rules," but the girls, who are "more tolerant in their attitude toward rules, more willing to make exceptions, and more easily reconciled to innovations."

Like the fifth-grade boys who "enjoyed the legal debates as much as they did the game itself," the Pharisees enjoyed their nitpicking of the law more than doing what the law required in human relationships. As Jesus rebuked them, "You give God one tenth even of the seasoning herbs, such as mint, dill, and cumin, but you neglect to obey the really important teachings of the Law, such as justice and mercy and honesty" (Matt 23:23). Like the girls, however, Jesus' ministry, in focusing on human hurts and needs before the Law, subordinated the continuation of the game (religion) to the continuation of the relationship with God and other human beings: "The sabbath was made for the good of man; man was not made for the sabbath. So the Son of Man is Lord of the Sabbath" (Mark 2:27–28).

With the coming of Jesus, God's presence and power on earth shifted from law to spirit—from objective standard to spirituality, from individual to community, from ritual to relationship. From this perspective, the "feminization of the church" is no recent phenomenon; it began when Jesus came to earth. For the basis of His mission was to break the chains with which our male fears had bound God, and to reorient us to a path which women already walked.

Certainly, spirit—like the wind, as Jesus declared—defies our human efforts to measure or objectify it. In this present age, when at best we see no more clearly than as a "dim image in a mirror," our natural human powers can never wholly perceive spirit accurately nor respond to it appropriately. And so we dare not abandon all written standards or hierarchies without inviting anarchy. Someone must maintain the institution, the religion, so that current-day revelation may be evaluated by checking it against the ancient witness.

Yet we cannot be so wed to an objective standard that we restrain and inhibit the Spirit from His mission of renewal. The question for men in the church today, therefore, is this: shall we confine ourselves to being the guardian enforcers of law and hierarchy, abdicating to women the Spirit's agenda of revelation and renewal?

Only those who know the rules of the game can play it well. Can we men, who have steadfastly maintained the rules, now dare to trust the Spirit to draw us beyond objective standards into relationship with the Living God and with one another—not only so that the rules are upheld, but so that the players may be revitalized and strengthened as a team?

May such courage be ours as men of God.

14

An Ancient Mama's Boy
Is Called Out:

Wrestling with the Father God for New Life

> The man said, "Your name will no longer be Jacob. You have struggled with God and with men, and you have won; so your name will be Israel" (Gen. 32:28).

EVERY TIME I READ about Jacob's wrestling with God in the river gorge, I can't help thinking of a dimly lit tavern in the small town of Saltillo, Mexico, and an elderly but sturdy, broad-shouldered man who sat across the table from me one day. I was a high school teacher then, studying Spanish for the summer, and out on the town for the evening.

Manuel, he said his name was, and he added that he'd been a boxer—just for a short while, years ago, when he'd been about my age. I nodded pleasantly, and as I began to try out my latest Spanish lesson on him, he suddenly leaned forward, planted his elbow squarely in the middle of our small wooden table, looked me in the eye, and opened a thick, muscular hand—a clear invitation to an arm-wrestling match. Surprised—and a little scared, too—I started to explain that we never did study arm-wrestling at my university, but when I leaned forward and tried to help my faltering Spanish along with a gesture, before I knew it he had enfolded my hand in his large grip, and was nudging me on.

Giving up on my Spanish, I took a deep breath and leaned into it, straining. Bottles wavered, glasses trembled, and in no time at all, my hand fell back.

I sat there, out of breath, and he let go. "I stop boxing very soon," Manuel declared, holding his hands out in front of him and spreading his fingers wide. "I became a wrestler." He curled his fingers as if grasping, and said, "I don't like to stand so far away, like the boxer. I like to get my fingers on the flesh and touch to the bone."

And so, in our story of Jacob at the river gorge, we've got another unlikely match-up, with a God who also likes to get His fingers on the flesh, and touch to the bone. It's an unlikely match simply because Jacob isn't the wrestling type. We see this in the stark contrast the biblical storyteller draws between Jacob and his rough-and-tough brother Esau:

> The time came for (Rebecca) to give birth, and she had twin sons. The first was reddish, and his skin was like a hairy robe, so he was named Esau. The second one was born holding on tightly to the heel of Esau, so he was named Jacob (Gen. 25:24–25).

In the ancient Hebrew culture a man's name carried with it his very essence and identity. No Hebrew parents chose a name for their baby just because it sounded nice, but only because the name fit that child. So the name Esau means "covering," to describe the baby's hairy body. The name Jacob, however, means "the one who grabs from behind"—that is, "the cheater," "the one who'll do anything to keep someone else from getting ahead of him." Jacob wanted to be the first-born himself, to get his father's blessing and inheritance; so he was grabbing Esau to pull him back so Jacob could come out of the womb first. In football parlance, Jacob would be "called for clipping," since fair play requires you to look your man in the eye before blocking him out.

And so, from the very first day of his life we see Jacob acting like a scoundrel carrying a Hebrew name that brands him—apparently forever—as the kind of person who "grabs you from behind."

For "the boys grew up," we read, "and Esau became a skilled hunter, a man who loved the outdoors, but Jacob was a quiet man who stayed at home" (Gen. 25:27).

No, Jacob wasn't out there on the open plains with muscles and rawhide and wild animals and the other men, growing strong and self-reliant. Jacob preferred the safer, more comfortable life at home. Clearly, this made him his mother's favorite, and later she schemes to steal his father's blessing for Jacob. Basically, Jacob was a "mama's boy"—at least until that strange and compelling night in the river gorge when Jacob's life took on a whole new perspective for us. On that night, he was being chased from behind by his angry uncle Laban, whom he had cheated out of an entire sheep herd. Then he was confronted ahead by his angry brother Esau, whom he had cheated out of the family birthright. On that night, the cheating, lying, conniving "one who grabs from behind" sent his family ahead to camp, and went alone down into the river gorge. There, a man who later identified himself as God, came forth to challenge Jacob.

At this point, we might want to reason that a kind and caring and understanding God might meet Jacob in a setting where he would feel comfortable: perhaps, God might suddenly create a few tents around Jacob, with some lounge chairs and amenities, to make him feel more at home.

But no. That's not the kind of God we're listening to here.

"For Jacob stayed behind, alone," we read. "Then a man came and wrestled with him until just before daybreak" (32:24).

A wrestling match! One-on-one, fingers on the flesh, touched to the bone! What a strange, dirty trick for God to play on this poor fellow! A wrestling match between the all powerful God who can move mountains and destroy armies, and the boy who hid out in the tents with his mother while his brother was out hunting for the dinner meat.

"The one who grabs from behind" wrestled face-to face with God! The one who stayed among the tents now wrestled out in the open, alone, with God!

Stranger still, we read that Jacob managed to get a hold on God—an armlock, maybe?—and he hangs on for dear life. Then God—in a move that would make any wrestler call "foul!"—punches Jacob in the thigh, throwing his leg out of joint. Straining, aching, Jacob cries out at last, "I won't let you go unless You bless me!"

And of course, the blessing comes. But such a blessing!

"What is your name?" God asks. And remembering here the Hebrew custom regarding names, the question becomes, "Who are you?"

When he hung on for dear life and answered, "I'm Jacob, the one who grabs from behind, the trickster, the con-man, the liar, the scared mama's boy"—*then* God said, "This is who you were; from now on, you will be Israel, the one who tries hard, and succeeds."

Jacob got a new name! And not just a new label on the jar, but a whole new jar itself, a whole new person, a transformation. No longer was he the cheater, the loser; now he was Israel: the struggler, the winner.

God had touched Jacob to the bone, at the very core of his identity.

And so the biblical storyteller speaks to us even today—so the God of Love reaches out and seizes and shakes us at the very core of our identities, before blessing us with new life. For if indeed God is the love we human beings are created from and the love that we feel for others and long for from others, then those who have ever loved someone else know that love always requires a struggle. And the struggle for love is against the Jacob in us.

The story of Jacob says that before we can love somebody else, or be loved by someone else, we must wrestle with that part of ourselves that gets scared when love starts breaking down our defenses. It's the part that would sooner put an armlock on love and force other folks to be what we want them to be, to get what we want from them. It's that part of us that's determined to save face and stay on top no matter how badly we hurt others—the part that sooner or later begins cheating or manipulating the persons we care about most.

And in this story of Israel's origin, of how the people of God were shaped, we see that the Spirit of the Father-God is no magic wand that whisks us off to a new world of honeymoons and overnight success. Rather, the Father-God of Love confronts each man in the deep river gorge of his inner darkness, somewhere between his self-centered dishonesties and the truth. And when the Father has finished with him, He leaves the man aching and limping alone after that truth which alone can restore him to his full and intended self.

For the Good News that we men long for today comes only in the terrifying, painful initiation of the Cross in which we die to our proud natural self and rise anew as sons of the Father-God. The Good News, in fact, is to feel God's grip on our flesh, to cry out our name in all its unworthiness, to feel the pain in our bones, to receive the blessing of newness as we let go, and at last, to follow.

May we be so blessed.

Epilogue:
The Mirror
of Truth [1]

Jesus said to them, "Come with me..." (Matt. 4:19).

ONCE UPON A TIME, a tiny, newborn lion cub was lying with his mother in the jungle, resting in the warmth of the sun and his mother's fur. Suddenly, without warning, a loud noise rang out among the trees and his mother jumped to her feet. Startled, the cub tumbled into a nearby brush, then watched as his mother fell to the ground and several other creatures, moving on only two legs, rushed in and seized her. Too frightened to move, he sat there, stunned, as the two-legged ones lifted his mother and disappeared into the forest.

A strange and fearful silence fell over the area, and for a whole day the little cub dared not move out from the brush where he hid. Finally, his stomach began to ache with hunger, and, seeing no movement in the area, he ventured out and walked unsteadily ahead, hoping to find something to eat.

After some time, he came to a clearing and peered out from behind a leafy bush. Before him, in the middle of a lush, green meadow, were many other creatures—on four legs, with white, curly-bush skins, their heads bent low as they seized the grass with their teeth and chewed it.

These creatures are eating, and they seem very peaceful, the cub thought to himself. *Maybe they'll let me join them.*

As he stepped out into the meadow, one of the larger creatures came over to greet him. At once, the cub poured out the sad story of his mother, and how hungry he was.

"You're welcome to stay and live with us," the creature said. "We're sheep, and we can teach you how to eat the grass."

The tired and lonely little cub was so encouraged by such warm hospitality that he thanked the sheep, and set about putting his teeth to the grass. Soon he noticed that the sheep had teeth that were different from his own; he had to work very hard to grasp the grass and chew it. Nevertheless, he was a hardy little fellow, and would not give up. Before long he had learned how to squeeze his jaws—painful though it was—so that he could pinch the grass and get it into his mouth.

In fact, he became so fond of the sheep and so used to their company that he also learned how to open his mouth and make a "baaa-a-a" sound; he even managed to prance somewhat with his wide, soft feet as they did with their small, hard hooves.

Several years passed, and though he could never manage to eat, speak, or walk quite as the sheep did, the lion cub still enjoyed being one of their family. In time, he even forgot his mother and the terror of his first days alive.

And then one bright and sunny day, while the lion was grazing peacefully with his sheep family in the meadow, a loud and terrifying shriek suddenly burst forth from the mother sheep. Startled, he and the others stopped their grazing and looked up in alarm. "Quick! Everyone into the forest at once!" the mother sheep shouted. And without thinking, all the others turned and followed her as she darted into the thicket.

The young lion naturally turned to follow the sheep—but as he did, a strange impulse stopped him. *What*, he wondered, *was everyone so frightened of?* As he stood alone in the meadow, the mother sheep screamed at him one last time: "Come with us immediately!" Again the lion turned—but again, he stopped. "It's too late!" the mother sheep shouted. "We must leave you behind!" And she disappeared into the woods.

Alone and uncertain in the stillness of the warm afternoon, the lion puzzled over this strange turn of events. Shrugging his shoulders, he turned away from the forest where the sheep had run, and was about to bend down for another tear at the grass when suddenly his head jerked upright. A cold shiver of terror raced through his body as there, heading straight toward him— unhurried but deliberate—came a huge and mighty creature un- like any he had ever seen.

Its feet were like huge, padded tree stumps; its teeth were long and sharp. *How in the world*, the lion wondered, *did this creature eat? Surely such teeth could not chew grass!* Behind the creature stretched a long, thick tail with a large tuft of hair at the end.

What seized the young lion's attention, however, was the huge bush of hair surrounding the creature's head and waving majestically in the afternoon breeze.

With its dark eyes riveted to his own, the creature lumbered toward the trembling young lion. The mother sheep, he realized in a moment of horror, was right. It was too late.

Yet he was struck by a strange inner sense that held him there, even in his terror: he did not really want to run away from the creature. Indeed, he couldn't take his eyes off it.

And then, at last, the creature stood before him. The young lion's legs were shaking as his wide eyes beheld this awesome figure.

"Follow me," the creature said, his deep voice rumbling like a stormy sky.

As the creature turned and walked away, the young lion hesitated. Where in the world would it take him? An impulse arose to look over his shoulder to where the sheep had disap- peared in the woods, but he checked it. And then, he stepped forward, following.

For some time, the creature walked silently ahead. At first, the young lion tried to walk in its footsteps, but his sheep-prance kept him from doing so. Before long, though, he found himself leaping, stretching with surprising ease so that at times he even "caught" the creature's wide-spaced footprints. Still, he could only wonder at how much smaller his own feet were.

Leaping this way, the young lion was drawn up short—and stumbled clumsily—when the creature stopped and looked over its shoulder at him. "Come here, beside me," it said.

Struggling quickly to right himself, the young lion stepped beside the creature, who now stood before a small pond deep in the forest.

"Look down," the creature intoned, its rumbling voice echoing amid the trees.

The young lion looked down. There, on the surface of the water, he saw a small creature beside a large one. Tentatively, he shook his head—and the head of the smaller creature shook too, stirring thin tufts of hair behind its ears.

Puzzled, he drew back.

And then it struck him.

Hesitantly but deliberately, he leaned close to the water and looked again.

Then slowly, he turned and looked at the creature towering silently above him.

After a moment, he turned again to the water and stared intently.

The forest hushed.

At last, trembling, the young lion beheld the creature beside him. Lifting his head, he leaned back and thrust his sharp teeth at the treetops:

"R-R-R-O-O-O-A-A-A-R-R-R!"

Look! The Lion from Judah's tribe, the great descendant of David, has won the victory . . . (Rev. 5:5).

Endnotes

Introduction: Recognizing the Wound

1. Howard Halpern, "Ill-Boding Male-Bashing Bonanza," *Los Angeles Times View Section*, 27 October 1986.
2. Ted Dobson, "Healing the Tear in the Masculine Soul," *SCRC Vision*, April, 1985.

1. The Lion Speaks

1. David W. Smith, *The Friendless American Male* (Ventura, CA: Regal Books, 1983).
2. Leanne Payne, *Crisis in Masculinity* (Westchester, IL: Crossway Books, 1986), 46.
3. B. W. Anderson, *The Unfolding Drama of the Bible* (New York: The Association Press, 1957), 46.

2. Out from the Womb

1. Thomas Verny, M.D., *The Secret Life of the Unborn Child* (New York: Summit Books, 1981).
2. Robert Ruark, *Reader's Digest* (July 1974):207–8.
3. Paul Olsen, *Sons and Mothers* (New York: Ballantine Books, 1981), 41.
4. Keith Thompson, "The Meaning of Being Male—A Conversation with Robert Bly," *L.A. Weekly* (August 5–11, 1983), 17.
5. *Ibid.*, 18.
6. *Ibid.*, 18.
7. Garrison Keillor, "Winter," *News from Lake Wobegon* tape (St. Paul, MN: Minnesota Public Radio).

4. She Left Me!

1. Thompson, "The Meaning of Being Male," 16.
2. *Ibid.*, 16.
3. *Ibid.*, 16.
4. Pierre Mornell, *Passive Men, Wild Women* (New York: Ballantine Books, 1980), 68.
5. *Ibid.*, 68–69.
6. *Ibid.*, 106.
7. Deborah Laake, "Wormboys: Is He a Wimp, Or Isn't He?," *Reader* [Los Angeles] (4 November 1983), 8.
8. *Ibid.*, 8.
9. *Ibid.*, 8.
10. *Ibid.*, 8.
11. Lynda J. Barry, "The Sensitive Male," *Esquire* (July 1984), 85.
12. Laake, "Wormboys," 14.

6. To Corral the Stallion

1. Juan Carlos Ortiz, "Do Willingly and Joyfully His Will," a teaching delivered 24 March 1987, San Pedro, CA.

7. Lost Among Men: A Nonpolitical View of Homosexuality

1. Thompson, "The Meaning of Being Male," 19.
2. Ray Loynd, "Stage Review: An Ellipsis of the Son in 'Mother Tongue'," *Los Angeles Times Calendar* (24 February 1988), 1, 4.
3. John and Paula Sandford, *The Transformation of the Inner Man* (South Plainfield, NJ: Bridge Publishing, Inc., 1982), 78.
4. Rita Bennett, *How to Pray for Inner Healing* (Old Tappan, NJ: Fleming H. Revell Company, 1983), 84.
5. Andy Comiskey, "Healing the Child Within," *Desert Stream Newsletter* (January–February, 1985), 1.
6. *Ibid.*, 2.
7. *Ibid.*, 2.
8. *Ibid.*, 2.
9. *Ibid.*, 3.
10. *Ibid.*, 3.
11. *Ibid.*, 8.
12. Ruth Carter Stapleton, *The Gift of Inner Healing* (Waco, TX: Word, 1976), 92.
13. *Ibid.*, 95.

14. Rita Bennett, *Emotionally Free* (Old Tappan, NJ: Fleming H. Revell Company, 1982), 160.
15. *Ibid.*, 161.
16. *Ibid.*, 163.
17. Leanne Payne, *Crisis in Masculinity* (Westchester, IL: Crossway Books, 1985), 19.
18. *Ibid.*, 19.
19. *Ibid.*, 26.
20. *Ibid.*, 28.
21. *Ibid.*, 20.
22. *Ibid.*, 16.
23. *Ibid.*, 13.

8. Warrior Redeemed

1. Garry Trudeau, "Doonesbury," *Los Angeles Times*, 4 January 1987.
2. Keith Thompson, "The Meaning of Being Male," 16.
3. *Ibid.*, 16.
4. *Ibid.*, 16.
5. George Leonard, "The Warrior," *Esquire* (July 1986), 64, 66.
6. *Ibid.*, 66.
7. *Ibid.*, 70.
8. *Ibid.*, 71.
9. *Ibid.*, 71.
10. *Ibid.*, 71.
11. *Ibid.*, 71.
12. "Sgt. Fury and His Howling Commandos," *Marvel Comics* (November 1970).
13. Doug Krikorian, "A.C. plugs religion into his successful career," *Los Angeles Herald Examiner* (5 May 1987), C2.
14. John and Paula Sandford, "Intercessory Prayer" (tape), Elijah House Ministries, Spokane, WA.
15. *Webster's New Twentieth Century Dictionary of the English Language Unabridged Second Edition* (London: Wm. Collins Publishers, Inc., 1979), 1593.
16. *The Heidelberg Catechism with Commentary* (New York: The Pilgrim Press, 1962), 131.

10. The Father and the Man: Of Sons and Daughters

1. Robert M. Herhold, *The Promise beyond the Pain* (Nashville: Abingdon, 1979), 77.

2. Madeleine L'Engle, *A Wrinkle in Time* (New York: Dell Publishing Company, 1962), 152.
3. *Ibid.*, 171–2.
4. *Ibid.*, 200.

11. To Know the Father

1. Chaim Potok, *The Chosen* (New York: Simon & Schuster, 1967).

12. Where Are All the Men?: Why Men Don't Come to Church

1. Sharon Mielke, "Church analyst says trends need serious attention: Low number of men and big churches is major problem in UMC, district and conference leaders told," *United Methodist Reporter* (10 September 1982), 1.
2. Ed Robb, "Is the Church Feminized? An Interview with Dr. Donald Joy," *Challenge to Evangelism Today*, Vol. 16, No. 2 (July/August 1983), 1.
3. Anne S. White, *Trial by Fire* (Kirkwood, MO: Impact Books, 1975), 102.
4. *Alcoholics Anonymous Blue Book* (New York: Alcoholics Anonymous World Services, Inc., 1976), 59.

13. Rational and Independent, Faithless and Alone

1. David W. Smith, *The Friendless American Male*, 50.
2. Carol Gilligan, *In a Different Voice* (Cambridge, MA: Harvard University Press, 1982), 6–7.
3. *Ibid.*, 8.
4. *Ibid.*, 46.
5. *Ibid.*, 9.
6. *Ibid.*, 10.

Epilogue: The Mirror of Truth

1. I heard this story some years ago at a conference, and have been unable to find its source.

GORDON DALBEY is an ordained United Church of Christ minister and a graduate of Duke University (B.A., mathematics), Stanford University (M.A., journalism), and Harvard Divinity School (M.Div.). While at Harvard he won the Billings Prize (preaching) in 1975 and 1977. His articles have appeared in a wide variety of publications, such as *Leadership, Catholic Digest, Christian Century, Reader's Digest, Christian Herald, America,* and the *Los Angeles Times.* He was a Peace Corps Volunteer in Nigeria, and has taught math, journalism, and English in high schools. He teaches and leads spiritual growth programs for local churches, denominational events, and other Christian groups.